ANTI-POSTONE

ANTI-POSTONE

ANTI-POSTONE

or, Why Moishe Postone's
Antisemitism Theory is
Wrong, but Effective

Michael Sommer

COSMONAUT PRESS

Published by Cosmonaut Press.
Cosmonaut Press is an imprint of Cosmonaut, Inc.

Editor: Alexander Gallus
Proofreader: Adam Gibson
Interior Design: Tobias Houlgate
Cover Design: Bijan Sharifi

ISBN 978-1-953273-05-5

This is an original print edition of *Anti-Postone*.

CONTENTS

TRANSLATOR'S PREFACE

The essay by Michael Sommer that I have translated into English for this publication first appeared in a German-language volume entitled *Antifa heisst Luftangriff* (Laika 2014, *Antifa means Air Raid*). A collection of texts by various authors, it criticized the degeneration of anti-fascism in Germany and in Austria from a left-wing endeavor into an ideology that is now fully affirmative of liberal capitalism and defends it against its various detractors. Sommer's contribution, "Falsch aber wirkungsvoll" ("Wrong but Effective"), analyzed and, in my view, very efficiently demolished the antisemitism theory of the Canadian academic Moishe Postone, which had provided some of the key concepts for the new German anti-fascism, both institutional and "militant," roughly since the turn of the century.

The central device of this system-friendly anti-fascism has been antisemitism charges — aimed usually not at fascists, but at the anti-capitalist left, and more recently also at Arab migrants and the German working class. Sommer argues in his essay that the critique offered by Postone's epigones "presents itself with the gesture of a theoretically upgraded anti-fascism, yet in reality pursues very little aside from accusing those of fascism who defend themselves against the ravages of capitalism today." As we will see, it also rests on theoretically unsustainable foundations and is therefore, plainly speaking, bunk.

When the essay was first published in Germany in 2014, Anglophone readers might have struggled to comprehend how an ostensibly radical German left could allow itself to be sidetracked into adopting essentially pro-capitalist and pro-imperialist positions in the name of resisting antisemitism. Had the text been made available to them at the time, the antics of Postonean "anti-fascists" described by Sommer in the opening pages would have been met with incredulity. German guilt may have been identified as the psychological motivating force, and the notion that "this could not happen here" would have prevailed especially among readers from the UK, where few self-identified socialists, with the notable exception of the Alliance for Workers' Liberty, were susceptible to the spectre of a rampant left antisemitism.

This can no longer be taken for granted. As I write, the UK boasts a rudderless left that has emerged from the demoralizing experience of supporting Jeremy Corbyn as Labour Party leader for a matter of almost five years. During this period, it was subjected to a systematic witch-hunt: from April 2016 right until Corbyn's general election defeat in December 2019, reports of "Labour antisemitism" were appearing in the British media almost on a daily basis, and suspensions, expulsions, and the public hounding of left-wingers were rife. The reasons for this are not difficult to fathom: here you had the potential party of government in the fifth-largest economy in the world, the heart of financial imperialism linked through a "special relationship" to the US (and thus to its key Middle Eastern ally Israel), suddenly led by an anti-war activist whom the capitalist class could only regard as unreliable. And so, a broad range of establishment forces found that it was in their common interest to stop Corbyn and his supporters. After successive ill-fated attempts to portray him as unpatriotic, an IRA sympathizer, a communist, and so on, these forces eventually stumbled upon the most effective weapon of all: antisemitism charges. They proved so effective precisely because antisemitism is considered today the most reprehensible vice, perhaps second only to pedophilia, by the vast majority of British society across the political spectrum. Few people, including on the far right, would want to be associated with it.

The disinformation and smear campaign that ensued was unprecedented in scope. Since instances of actual antisemitic sentiment in the Labour Party were rare, social media accounts were trawled going back many years, off-hand comments turned and twisted and "antisemitic tropes" found everywhere — the beauty of the tactic being that almost any accusation of corruption, scheming, or collusion with the enemy can be read as an "antisemitic trope," even when it is a statement of fact.[1]

The longer the campaign went on, the more the narrative of an epidemic of antisemitism in Labour made inroads into parts of the British left itself. While a sheepish silence was the response of its majority to the witch-hunt — better to throw comrades to the wolves than "die on that

---

[1]   The best-known case in this regard was probably the anti-racist activist Marc Wadsworth, who in 2018 was expelled from the Labour Party for accusing the Labour MP Ruth Smeeth for working "hand-in-hand" with the *Daily Telegraph*. Smeeth happened to be Jewish and, more to the point, was part of the anti-Corbyn Labour right — so Wadsworth's remark was construed as an "antisemitic trope." In more recent cases, such as that of the Bristol university lecturer David Miller, charges of "dishonesty" and "racism" against pro-Israel organizations have also been identified as "antisemitic tropes" by some — see *Jewish News* article of 19 Feb 2021 at https://jewishnews.timesofisrael.com/pressure-mounts-on-bristol-uni-over-academic-accused-of-antisemitic-tropes/.

hill" — some discernibly began to wonder whether the left *didn't* have an antisemitism problem, after all. Soon you could hear certain activists demanding that "we start from anti-racism" and take the accusations seriously, no matter where they emanated from — or to what ends they were being employed.

In Britain it was not misplaced guilt that rendered the left incapable of defending itself, but its diminishing ability to see the bigger picture beyond a multitude of causes and concerns, coupled with its unwillingness to challenge the subjective standpoints of professed spokespeople for identity groups — read: its intersectionality. Moreover, the left did not recognize that its enemies had learned to avail themselves of the left's own weapons, including its language, in order to attack, divide, and demobilize it.

In November 2020, the Labour MP Nadia Whittome, who is politically close to the Alliance for Workers' Liberty, made a rare explicit mention of Postone in an article for *LabourList*, in which she reprimanded Jeremy Corbyn for noting that Labour antisemitism had been "overstated."[2,3] Various themes also typical of Postonean "anti-fas-

---

2   Nadia Whittome, "Labour antisemitism must be confronted — with nuance, clarity and empathy," *LabourList*, Nov. 29, 2020, https://labourlist.org/2020/11/labour-antisemitism-must-be-confronted-with-nuance-clarity-and-empathy/.

3   Martin Thomas and other Alliance for Workers' Liberty

cism" have been invoked in a much cruder fashion not by left-wingers, but by establishment figures. Thus Siobhain Mcdonagh, the Labour MP for Mitcham and Morden, remarked in an interview with BBC Radio Four that it is "part of hard left politics to be against capitalists and to see Jewish people as the financiers of capital. Ergo you are anti-Jewish people."[4] And in October 2020, the U.S. Department of State organized an international conference on internet antisemitism. There, the attempt was made to subsume all politics that pose a nuisance to US foreign policy — far-left, far-right, and Islamist — as "antisemitic," while guests such as the former Labour MP Luciana Berger and the British government's "antisemitism Tsar," John Mann, expounded on anti-capitalism and antisemitism.[5]

---

members have written favorably on Postone and interviewed him. See, e.g., "Postone, capitalism, and the working class" at https://www.workersliberty.org/story/2018-12-30/postone-capitalism-and-working-class, "Anti-semitism and reactionary anti-capitalism" at https://www.workersliberty.org/story/2017-07-26/anti-semitism-and-reactionary-anti-capitalism, and "Moishe Postone 1942-2018" at https://www.workersliberty.org/story/2018-03-28/moishe-postone-1942-2018.

4   "Siobhain McDonagh links anti-capitalism to antisemitism in Labour," *LabourList*, Mar. 4 2019, https://labourlist.org/2019/03/siobhain-mcdonagh-links-anti-capitalism-to-antisemitism-in-labour/.

5   Luciana Berger, "My Story — 'Under Attack,'" (presentation, U.S. Department of State Conference on Internet Anti-Semitism, Oct. 21, 2020), https://2017-2021.state.gov/anti-semitism-conference-2020/my-story-under-attack/index.html.

In a March 2019 article for the *Financial Times*, the Blair-ite political advisor to the Labour Party John McTernan made a statement that is worth quoting at length:

> As the historian Deborah Lipstadt points out, anti-Semitic tropes share three elements: money or finance is always in the mix; an acknowledged cleverness that is also seen as conniving; and, power — particularly a power to manipulate more powerful entities. All of these feature in the criticism of Israel and the so-called Israel lobby. They can be easily moulded into a critique of capitalism, too. Rhetoric about the 1 per cent and economic inequality has the same underlying theme — a small group of very rich people who cleverly manipulate others to defend their interests. So anti-capitalism masks and normalises anti-Semitism.[6]

Of course, this is not to say that Siobhain McDonagh or John McTernan are Postone disciples, but they do rehash popular versions of his "insights" picked up second-hand. What's more, the antisemitism campaign, although originally targeting the left, has paradoxically opened up some of its softer sections to such ideas. It is not inconceivable, then, that Postone's theses will finally fall on fertile ground in Britain too, offering a superficially Marxist theoretical framework for a left that is temporarily defeated and unwilling to "die on that hill" next time around. In the long

---

6   John McTernan, "Labour's mistake is to believe there are no enemies to the left," *Financial Times*, Mar. 1 2019, https://www.ft.com/content/2448aafc-3b89-11e9-9988-28303f70fcff.

run, this could prove a far greater success for the right than the expulsions of left-wingers from the Labour Party were.[7]

This booklet cannot stop the left from absorbing the bourgeois ideology of its time. But I hope it will make it a great deal harder for those peddling Postonean sophistries to justify them theoretically, let alone be taken seriously when touting them as Marxist — or as in any way serving human liberation. Above all, I hope that Sommer's vivid exposure of these arguments will contribute toward inoculating the international left against the extreme political

---

7   Indeed, Matt Bolton and Frederick Harry Pitts's *Corbynism: A Critical Approach* (Emerald Publishing, 2018) attempted to add some "academic Marxist" muscle to the witch-hunt — the text was substantially informed by Postone's antisemitism theory and in fact dedicated to his memory. As I finish writing this preface, I receive news that the snappily named No Pasaran Press is about to publish a Daniel Randall book entitled *Confronting Antisemitism on the Left: Arguments for Socialists*. Randall is a Labour Party member and Alliance for Workers' Liberty supporter who frequently cites Moishe Postone's work as crucially informing his understanding of antisemitism. No Pasaran Press presents itself as a "left-wing activist collective" — see https://www.nopasaran.media. However, a cursory check in the British government's business directory reveals that it is run by Baron Jonathan Mendelsohn, a life peer in the House of Lords who is also on the board of directors in the Blairite Labour think tank Progress, the former chair of Labour Friends of Israel, and involved in a variety of other pro-Israel organizations. Another No Pasaran Press publication, Ben Freeman's *Jewish Pride*, which explicitly sets out to counter the growing trend of left-wing anti-Zionism among young diaspora Jews, was launched at the Menachem Begin Heritage Center in Jerusalem. For No Pasaran Press business information, see https://find-and-update.company-information.service.gov.uk/company/11938098/officers.

degeneration that we have seen occur in Germany. Some topical references found in Sommer's text, such as those to the Blockupy protests of 2013, may now seem dated — but his analysis of this pseudo-scientific variety of "anti-antisemitism" remains essential.

— Maciej Zurowski
Taranto, August 2021

Introduction

Comrade Zurowski's translator's preface indicates why it is desirable to translate Michael Sommer's "Anti-Postone." Witch-hunting anti-capitalism as antisemitic, and therefore "fascist," began as a *significant* tendency in Germany around the time of the 1989 reunification,[1] and was intensified there with the rise of Die Linke after 2007 (with the practical result of capturing Die Linke for US Middle-East policy).[2] It spread beyond Germany with the campaign to reverse the continental European public opposition to the invasion of Iraq, reflected (after a tortuous process) in the

---

1   Convenient discussion in Wikipedia, "Anti-Germans" https://en.wikipedia.org/wiki/Anti-Germans_(political_ current). It should be noted that in the USA, efforts to illegalize and no-platform Palestine solidarity initiatives go back to the 1970s: e.g. https://www.bis.doc.gov/index.php/enforcement/oac, cited in Anon., *Note,* "Wielding Anti-discrimination Law to Suppress the Movement for Palestinian Rights" 133 *Harv. L. Rev.* 1360 (2020) at n. 33.
2   See e.g. https://www.die-linke.de/partei/parteidemokratie/ parteivorstand/parteivorstand/detail/stoppt-die-gewalt-in-israel-und-palaestina/ (15 May 2021); https://www. jns.org/german-politicians-sound-unprecedented-pro-israel-rhetoric-at-berlin-rally/ (25 May 2021).

intergovernmental International Holocaust Remembrance Alliance 2016 Working Definition of Antisemitism.[3]

With the 2015 election of Jeremy Corbyn, a central leader of the Stop the War Campaign, to the leadership of the British Labour Party, a variety of smears were attempted: e.g., Corbyn was said to be an agent of the Czech bureaucratic regime, and/or a friend of terrorists, and/or the left was claimed to be male-chauvinist. In 2016 this approach failed to deliver a successful parliamentary-Labour coup against Corbyn, and in 2017 it failed to deliver a majority for the Conservatives. But the antisemitism smear campaign continued without let-up, and the failure of the Corbyn leadership to actively denounce it or defend those targeted, together with the leadership's allowing itself to be drawn into the trap of supporting "Conservative Remainer" initiatives in parliament (attempts to use procedural maneuvers to prevent British exit from the EU), allowed a smashing victory for the Tories in December 2019. This has been followed by a yet-more-aggressive deployment of the "antisemitism" defamation campaign,

---

3   https://www.holocaustremembrance.com/resources/working-definitions-charters/working-definition-antisemitism. For the earlier stages of production, beginning with the American Jewish Committee and the European Union Monitoring Committee, see https://www.ohchr.org/Documents/Issues/Religion/Submissions/JBI-Annex1.pdf.

to ground an ongoing programme of expulsions, by the new Labour leadership under securocrat (former Director of Public Prosecutions) Sir Keir Starmer.

In the UK, the *particular form* of "Frankfurt School" narrative provided by Postone's article is relatively weak. The Labour right by and large merely argue from ordinary western and UK loyalism, and *parrot* without much explanation the idea that anti-zionism is *ipso facto* antisemitism. The "Eustonites" proceeded fairly straightforwardly from Eurocommunism to common or garden "progressive" liberalism and thence to a revival of late 19th-early 20th century "Liberal imperialism."[4] The Matgamna-ites (*Socialist Organiser*, more recently Alliance for Workers' Liberty) moved between 1979 and 1983 from the "anti-Pabloite Trotskyist" dogma that "Stalinism is counter-revolutionary through and through," to Max Schachtman-style "third campism," and thus to "Soviet imperialism" and hence to anti-anti-imperialism.[5]

---

4   Convenient outline reference at Wikipedia "Euston Manifesto" https://en.wikipedia.org/wiki/Euston_Manifesto. On "Liberal imperialism" HCG Matthew, *The Liberal Imperialists. The Ideas and Politics of a Post-Gladstonian Élite* (Oxford: Oxford University Press, 1973).

5   As a contemporary outside observer of this change, it *seems* to me that the reason is that the Mandelite Trotskyist International Marxist Group-Socialist League in 1980 pulled out of student politics in order to conduct a "turn to industry." The Matgamna-ites saw a gap in the political market, and moved into student politics. But as a purely British group, they did

The underlying reason for the difference is probably that the purchase of "critical theory" in the British academic left is also weak.[6] Nonetheless, vulgarized versions of Postone's argument have appeared in Britain.[7] In North America, "critical theory" has more purchase — and Postone's article is more celebrated.

Michael Sommer provides a very strong systematic critique of the intellectual deficiencies of Postone's article. Similar deficiencies affect more generally Postone's larger work *Time, Labour and Social Domination*.[8] Two sympathetic "third camp" left reviewers of *TLSD*, Martin Thomas of the AWL and left communist Loren Goldner, drew attention, for example, to Postone's radical lack of engagement with the leftist literature critical of the USSR; Gold-

---

not have the Mandelites' "unique selling point," against the larger Socialist Workers' Party, of the Fourth International. To fill this gap, they allied with the Union of Jewish Societies against the SWP's support for "no platform for Zionists." This position was correct in itself (no-platforming does not suppress fascism, but merely hands weapons to the state; "no platform for racists" lacked even the sort-of justification of "no platform for fascists"). But since the Matgamna-ites *supported* (and still support) "no platform for fascists" they needed to reverse their pre-existing line on "anti-imperialism" if they were to justify their bloc with the J-Socs.

6   On the limited influence of the Frankfurt School in Britain see e.g., Douglas Kellner https://pages.gseis.ucla.edu/faculty/kellner/Illumina%20Folder/kell16.htm; Tom Steele, "Critical Theory and British Cultural Studies" *Counterpoints*, Vol. 168, (2003), pp. 222-237.

7   E.g., https://labourlist.org/2019/03/siobhain-mcdonagh-links-anti-capitalism-to-antisemitism-in-labour/.

8   Cambridge UP 1991.

ner also pointed out that Postone offered a radically selective quotation (of a passage Marx anyhow deleted from the final, French, edition of *Capital*) to be a central element of his case for capital as a system of "abstract" domination.[9] It can be added, again merely for example, that at pg. 4 of *TLSD* Postone attributed to Marx the view that labor is (under capitalism) "the source of all wealth" — a view that Marx explicitly denounced in the *Critique of the Gotha Progamme*.[10] There are a variety of other defects; in sum, it is pretty clear there is no serious reason to attribute to Marx what Postone calls "Marx's mature critical theory," since Marx down to his death maintained claims clearly opposed to Postone's interpretation. It thus equally seems likely that Cambridge University Press published *TLSD* in 1991 not for the merits of its "Marx scholarship" as scholarship, which is seriously weak, but for the congeniality of its central political conclusions — the rejection of any class politics — to those who advised the press to publish in the "moment" after the collapse of the eastern European bureaucratic regimes in 1989.

---

9   Thomas (writing actually after Postone's death) https:// www.workersliberty.org/story/2018-12-30/postone-cap-italism-and-working-class; Goldner, http://breaktheir-haughtypower.org/review-time-labor-and-social-domina-tion-by-moishe-postone/, the individual point at nr. 1.

10   https://www.marxists.org/archive/marx/works/1875/go-tha/ch01.htm — the very first paragraph of the text.

It may be useful to add here, to Sommer's substantive critique of Postone on antisemitism and of the epigones of this article, a little about the possible backgrounds to Postone's argument; on the one side, on the issue of antisemitism and the 1970s; on the other, the background to Postone's theoretical framework in the appropriation of the ideas of the "Frankfurt School" by the German and American SDS groups (Sozialistische Deutsche Studentenbund; Students for a Democratic Society) in the 1960s.

Antisemitism

All ideologies need something to give them a degree of plausibility. There is, for example, no known religion or political credo which asserts that the sun rises in the west and sets in the east. The ideology of Postone's article is about antisemitism as a mode of figuring *capitalism as such*, which is identified with "industrial modernity" and — in the move-too-far which is central to Sommer's critiques of Postone and his epigones — with "abstraction" considered as a property of capitalism as a social formation as such.

The rational core of this Postonean ideology is that in "classical" late nineteenth century antisemitism (as Sommer points out) money and finance capital is figured as "the Jew" and "unproductive," as opposed to the potentially virtuous, "productive," and "national" industrial capital. Postone adopts some of the evidence of this trope, but denies the opposition, projecting the antisemites' endorsement of industrial *capital* onto industrial *labor*. At least part of the background to this choice is Postone's prior rejection of class politics, which emerges from his SDS-Frankfurt School background — to be discussed later. However, Postone's claimed evidence for the choice is that the Nazis claimed that Marxism and Communism were "Jewish"; and the particularity of the Jewish Holocaust, as the only case of sustained efforts to eradicate a whole culture, which (it is said) cannot be explained by capitalist (or state) interests.[11]

The first of these arguments is trivially useless: the core of classical antisemitism was Catholic Social Teaching, and it was already directed from the 1880s as much against social-democracy as against liberalism.[12] The political objection to "money capital" was, in fact, older within capitalism, forming the basis of Tory objections to the "Jew Bill" (for naturalization of wealthy Jewish immigrants) of 1753 — and before that to the

---

11   In the version in *New German Critique* No. 19 (Dec 1980), 97-115, at 108, 105.
12   David I. Kertzer, *Unholy War: The Vatican's Role in the Rise of Modern Anti-Semitism* (Macmillan 2002).

political role of the supposedly unstable and non-national "moneyed interest" (as opposed to the virtuous and national "landed interest") in the 1690s-1700s.[13] The argument is from the national, eliding the actual clerical-traditional interest; and this argument is as much an objection against the internationalism of the Second and Third Internationals as against the Jews as a non-national group, and so on. The organic unity of the nation is strikingly downplayed from Postone's account of antisemitism, but strikingly present in actual antisemitisms, "national socialism" and Stalinist campaigns against "cosmopolitanism" included.

The second point is more important: it is a variant on "Holocaust uniqueness," which, though it had a limited constituency before the 1970s, became much more widely publicized from the 1970s.[14] Postone's starting point,

---

13   Jew Bill: e.g., Avinoam Yuval-Naeh "The 1753 Jewish Naturalization Bill and the Polemic over Credit," *Journal of British Studies* 57, (2018): 467–492. "Landed" and "moneyed" interests: e.g., Richard I. Cook, *Jonathan Swift as a Tory Pamphleteer* (University of Washington Press, 1967). The discourse persisted in Burke's Reflections on the Revolution in France and down to the Commons debate in 1854 on the repeal of the Usury Acts: https://api.parliament.uk/historic-hansard/commons/1854/aug/04/usury-laws-repeal-bill.

14   Norman Finkelstein, *The Holocaust Industry*, 2nd edition (New York: Verso, 2014), Ch 2. The objections which have been made to Finkelstein's argument, so far as these objections have a good-faith character, do not displace this dating point.

in fact, is one of the products of this radical expansion of "Holocaust culture": the impact in Germany of the US TV mini-series *Holocaust*.[15]

Whatever the merits of "Holocaust uniqueness" in general, Postone's use of it is not historically defensible. The attempt to extirpate a whole minority ethno-religious-culture or cultures, considered as polluting the nation, was made in Spanish 17th century *limpieza di sangre* projects; this did not create a genocide merely because at the time the technology did not exist to close borders.[16] Closer in time to the Holocaust, the Armenian genocide of 1915-17 certainly had the object of purifying the Turkish nation, and did largely wipe out the Armenian minority in Turkey, with a substantially lower technical base than 1940s Germany.[17] Similar national-social purification aims were present in Young Turk and Kemalist policy towards the Anatolian Greeks during and after World War I, though here the relation of forces forced mass deportations rather than mass killings.[18]

---

15   Summary account of the miniseries and its reception at https://en.wikipedia.org/wiki/Holocaust_(miniseries).

16   Discussion e.g., in François Soyer, *Antisemitic Conspiracy Theories in the Early Modern Iberian World*, Brill 2019.

17   Discussion e.g., Donald Bloxham, "The Armenian Genocide of 1915-1916: Cumulative Radicalization and the Development of a Destruction Policy," *Past & Present*, No. 181 (Nov. 2003), 141-191.

18   Discussion e.g., Sarah Shields, "The Greek-Turkish Popu-

Postone was writing at a time when there were in circulation both extensive propaganda exploitation of "antisemitism" by the US and its Israeli client, and *actual* antisemitic discourses. The propaganda aspect was "new antisemitism," an idea promoted by Israeli Foreign Minister Abba Eban in 1973 and enthusiastically taken up by US writers. The idea was that "Israel is the Jew of the nations," i.e., that the hostility of the left to the Israeli state was, as such, discriminatory against Jews. The problem with this line was that even if the 1967 war *was* really "pre-emptive self-defense" at its start, by annexing East Jerusalem and embarking on settlements in the occupied territories, Israel retrospectively became a "trespasser *ab initio*" and converted the war into a war of aggression in violation of the Nuremberg Principles and UN Charter. Israel was therefore not claiming only the rights allowed to all states/ peoples, but a special right to territorial expansionism *not* available to other states or peoples. General perception of this was reflected not only in immediate sympathy for the Palestinians, but also in a widespread leftist retrospective negative re-evaluation of 1948.

The core driver of the actual circulation of antisemitic

lation Exchange," *Middle East Report* 267 (Summer 2013) https://merip.org/2013/06/the-greek-turkish-population-exchange/.

ideas was also the Israel-Palestine issue. The underlying problem was that the US state pretended not to support its Israeli client and to act as an "honest broker" between Israel and the Arab states, and between Israel and the Palestinians. In fact, however, the US had and has geo-political interests in veto control of the Middle East as an oil-producing area, in order to hold *potential* rivals in military subordination by controlling access to oil, which powers armed forces. These interests led the Kennedy administration to introduce large-scale US military aid to Israel, and ever since then US policy has been governed by maintaining Israel's "qualitative military edge" over its neighbors.[19]

The flat conflict between what the US *says*, about pursuing "peace," what it *doesn't say*, by failing to openly avow its security interests in veto control of the region, and what it *does*, by pretty much consistently backing Israel, naturally produces theories according to which the US's practice

---

19   "U.S. Foreign Policy and Israel's Qualitative Military Edge: The Need for a Common Vision," *The Washington Institute for Near East Policy*, Jan 24, 2008, https://www.washingtoninstitute.org/policy-analysis/us-foreign-policy-and-israels-qualitative-military-edge-need-common-vision.   This dates at least the expression to after the 1967 war; but the decisive steps taken by the Kennedy administration, as part of Cold War policy, are discussed by Vaughn P. Shannon, *Balancing Act: US Foreign Policy and the Arab-Israeli Conflict* (Ashgate, 2003; Kindle edition, 2020) Ch 2, text at nn. 45-49.

is really governed not by US interests but by the "Zionist lobby" — Israeli tail wags American dog,[20] or, worse, that Washington is being run by an international Jewish conspiracy or "Jewish-capitalist class."[21] This is, broadly, the context of the expansion of European antisemitic ideas in the middle east.[22]

The Stalinist bureaucracy in the USSR, moreover, in the wake of the 1967 war revived the nationalist antisemitism of the late Stalin years.[23] And it has to be noticed that Hilferding's *Finance Capital*, heavily deployed by Lenin in *Imperialism, the Highest Stage of Capitalism*, the latter a text which was very influential on the left in the later 1960s to 1970s, slips somewhat into the frame of finance = unproductive, so as to be susceptible of a Catholic Social Teaching reading; not, in fact, Marx's view (for which finance is

---

20 Discussion by Moshé Machover, "Imperialism, Palestine and Israel," *Weekly Worker*, Sep 5 2007; id., "A Very Special Relationship," The Project, May 2 2015, https://www.socialist-project.org/international/a-very-special-relationship/.

21 For a (trivial) example, https://commexplor.com/2014/09/06/draft-theses-on-the-jews-and-modern-imperialism/.

22 Discussion e.g., Norman A. Stillman, "New Attitudes toward the Jew in the Arab World," *Jewish Social Studies*, Vol. 37 (1975), 197-204.

23 Cf. L. Trotsky, "Thermidor and anti-semitism" (1937) https://www.marxists.org/archive/trotsky/1937/02/therm.htm; Konstantin Azadovskii and Boris Egorov, "From Anti-Westernism to Anti-Semitism," *Journal of Cold War Studies*, vol 4 (2002), 66-80; William Korey, "The Origins and Development of Soviet Anti-Semitism: An Analysis," *Slavic Review*, vol. 31, (1972), 111-135.

a necessary phase or component of the circuit of capital, merely separated-off to accelerate returns).[24]

The 1967 war also took place towards the end of the period of "demonstrative direct actions" by the New Left, and not long before the British scuttle out of Aden (November 1967) and the Tet Offensive in Vietnam (starting 31 January 1968). The Palestinians therefore — like very many radicals all around the world — hoped that the methods of guerrilla struggle and "prolonged people's war" could win: in their case, bring down the Zionist state. But cross-border raiding failed: Israel's "qualitative military edge" was too strong. Palestinian organizations therefore turned to "demonstrative" terror against softer Israeli-overseas targets.[25] But the extent of Israeli state involvement in Jewish organizations internationally is such that it was fatally easy to slide from targeting Israeli overseas assets, to targeting simply Jewish assets.[26] We arrive

24   David Harvey, *The Limits to Capital* (new ed. Verso 2006) Ch 10; Matari Pierre Manigat, "Finance Capital and Financialization: A Comparative Reading of Marx and Hilferding" https://journals.openedition.org/oeconomia/9122 (2020).
25   On New Left "demonstrative actions": Todd Gitlin, *The Whole World is Watching: Mass Media in the Making and Unmaking of the New Left*, (2003 ed., U Cal Press) is useful. Palestinian guerrilla efforts: convenient narrative in Daniel L. Byman "The 1967 War and the birth of international terrorism," Brookings (blog), May 30, 2017, https://www.brookings.edu/blog/markaz/2017/05/30/the-1967-war-and-the-birth-of-international-terrorism/.
26   I should add that this is not a point specific to Israel. States

here at Postone's reference to the 1976 Entebbe hijacking and IDF hostage rescue, involving the Popular Front for the Liberation of Palestine working with the German far-left terrorist *Revolutionäre Zellen* — who Postone argues inverted German guilt for the Holocaust.[27]

My point here is not to make antisemitic ideas into some sort of sin against the Holy Ghost. Not all antisemitic ideas inexorably produce the Holocaust. But what I have just been discussing in relation to left politics and "anti-imperialism" is largely antediluvian 1970s politics, which is antediluvian to modern eyes because of its radical failure. The point is then, in fact, the opposite of Postone's anti-class politics argument: the fundamental problem with "left antisemitism" is that it places confidence in some section of the capitalist class or the state bureaucracy: in this case, the nationalists/traditionalists. Those who hold out hopes for the populism of the nationalists/traditionalists will inevitably be betrayed, as happened to the large majority of the Iranian left in 1979–81, and more recently to those who imagined the Muslim

generally have so much more resources available than voluntary associations that they will naturally tend, in the absence of clear resistance to accepting state funding, to "take over" voluntary associations for their own ends. Thus the "official" communist parties and the USSR.

27   Above n. 11, 103-104.

Brotherhood as an alternative to the military regime in Egypt, or held out hope in Donald Trump to restore the "rustbelt."

But this is also a problem with the other side of the coin, which is to attach the left to liberalism. "New Labour" turned out to be a combination of privatization, strong-state measures, and war abroad. Voting for "hope" in the elections of Obama achieved... more drone assassinations, and the most minimalist possible health reform. Choosing Hilary Clinton as the "electable" Democrat led to the election of Trump. But hitching the left's wagon to the liberals was already the logic of Postone's sub-Frankfurt-school theoretical approach.

The Frankfurt School and the 1960s New Left

One might easily assume that Postone was writing pure theory without political antecedents and involvements (beyond the critique of "traditional Marxism"). But this is misleading — or, rather, reflects the fact that the failure of the political trend in which Postone was involved was so complete that pretty much nothing is left except academic traces. This trend is the German and American SDS groups.

Postone's connection is not entirely clear in materials online, but can pretty reasonably be inferred from the people (other than his teachers) he credited in the acknowledgements to *TLSD* (at xi) — in particular his contemporary and coauthor of his earliest published piece, Helmut Reinicke, who was active in the US civil rights movement in 1963-64, and in German SDS from 1965; Wolfram Wolfer-Melior, author of a 1981 introduction to a reprint of SDS-er Rudi Dutschke on organization; and Dan Diner, who "came of political age within the New Left of the 1960s."[28] The relationship is also visible in Postone's early writing for the journal *Telos*, originally launched in 1968 as a "new left theory journal."[29] And it is visible in the structure and substance of the arguments.

---

28   Reinicke's Wikipedia page, https://de.wikipedia.org/wiki/ Helmut_Reinicke; Wolfer-Melior, "Organisation als Problem revolutionärer Existenz," in Basisgruppen, Internationalismus-Tage Tübingen 11 Dez bis 13 Dez 1981, (Köln/ Bonn 1981); on Diner, Jeffrey Herf, "The Struggle continues," New Republic Aug 5 2002, https://newrepublic.com/article/66401/the-struggle-continues.

29   Postone in *Telos*: "On Nicolaus 'Introduction' to the Grundrisse," *Telos* 1974 no. 22 130-148; 'Revolt im bürgerliche Erbe: Gebrauchswert und Mikrologie' *Telos* 1976, 239-245'; John Alt, 'Radical and Conservative Critique: A Conference Report' *Telos* 1985 no. 63 121-138 (Postone's commentary on papers and discussion on it at 134-35). On the origins of *Telos*, the quote here is from http://kennethandersonlawofwar. blogspot.com/2007/11/telos-critical-theory-journal-and-its. html; cf also Danny Postel, 'The metamorphosis of Telos' *In these Times* 1991, http://dev.autonomedia.org/node/3049; Timothy Luke, 'The Trek with Telos' https://fastcapitalism. uta.edu/1_2/luke.html.

In one of his interviews, Postone said that he radical-
ized in the early-mid 1960s, which would place him in the
"high tide" of SDS:

> I was a student, a very long time ago, in the fabled six-
> ties, and like many students of that generation, I was in some
> general ways politically progressive. There was a strange
> — retrospectively very strange — sense of optimism, that
> was fairly broad and that perhaps was associated with the
> election of John Kennedy, which seem to have changed the
> general atmosphere in the country, on the one hand, and the
> civil rights movement, on the other. Many of us strongly felt
> that segregation and racism were not just wrong, but were
> on the losing end of history. That, in a sense, went along
> with a kind of optimism.[30]

The mid-60s SDS groups had a basic common ideological aspect. This was the influence of left-Weberian sociol-
ogist C. Wright Mills, and of Frankfurt School writer Her-
bert Marcuse's *One-Dimensional Man* (1964). The general
frame was the (Weberian) characterization of the social
problem as "industrial rationality" ("east" and "west") and

---

30   https://ucpr.blog/2018/09/13/an-interview-with-moishe-po-
stone-marx-capitalism-and-the-possibility-of-activism-to-
day/. Two other interviews gave a date of 1969: https://
www.workersliberty.org/story/2018-12-30/postone-capi-
talism-and-working-class, and https://www.chicagomaroon.
com/article/2018/10/19/moishe-postone-marxist-scholar-so-
cial-theorist-194/. Postone graduated with a BSc in Biochemis-
try in 1963, and returned to Chicago University to study history
at Masters' level in 1965 or 1966 (MA 1967; ABD 1969). This
history suggests that the earlier date in the UCPR blog interview
is the right one.

rejection of the idea of the leading role of the working class in the emancipation of humanity, in favor of a leading role for intellectuals or students, or for those at the margins.[31]

In spite of the considerable mid-60s success of SDS and similar projects, by 1969 this strategic conception was busted. "Wildcat strikes" beginning in the mid-60s seriously undermined the idea that the working class was fully integrated in capitalist society, and May '68, the "creeping May" in Italy, and the late 1960s – early 1970s strike wave in Britain, knocked it on the head. Meanwhile, the Chinese Cultural Revolution gave a spurious new image of radicalism to Maoism, while Vietnam and other events added to the apparent plausibility of the "prolonged people's war" perspective. In 1969, both US and German SDS split and collapsed, leaving behind some Maoist and sub-Maoist groups, famously some terrorists (the Weather Underground in the US and the Red Army Fraction in Germany) — but nothing but political gravel out of the

---

31   E.g., Wright Mills's 1960 *Letter to the New Left* https://www.marxists.org/subject/humanism/mills-c-wright/letter-new-left.htm; Marcuse, *One Dimensional Man*, Ch 2 (https://www.marxists.org/ebooks/marcuse/one-dimensional-man.htm#s2). More general discussion of the politics of the two SDSs in e.g., Martin Klimke, *The Other Alliance: Student Protest in West Germany and the United States in the Global Sixties* (Princeton UP, 2010); Paul Heideman, "Half the Way with Mao Zedong," *Jacobin*. 23 May 2018, https://jacobinmag.com/2018/05/half-the-way-with-mao-zedong/.

Marcusian–Millsian cores.[32] Part of that gravel must have been the — presumably informal — group working on Frankfurt School-theory in the 1970s which is reflected in Postone's co-authorships and his acknowledgements to Germans for discussion and support in *TLSD*.

It is thus clear that Postone's rejection of class politics, explicit in *TLSD* and implicit in the antisemitism article, is not a *conclusion* from this work, but rather a *dogmatic presupposition* of it, derived from the SDS milieux and their appropriations of Marcuse, Wright Mills, and so on. This is, in fact, already visible in the 1974 Postone-Reinicke critique of Nicolaus's introduction to his translation of Marx's *Grundrisse*, which is the first piece in the Postone corpus:

> The Grundrisse has become known [...] also when the revolt of the 1960s *has largely subsided* and when increasing numbers of young leftists turn to a traditional Marxist theory and practice whose inadequacies *had been practically demonstrated by the newer forms of struggle*.[33]

These statements, as written in 1973–74 (thus, for example, published in the midst of the Portuguese revolution) could only make sense if "revolt" meant the 1960s

---

32   Third-camp Trotskyist perspective on the American split from the "Independent Socialist Clubs" https://www.workersliberty.org/story/2019-11-13/split-sds. Feminist perspective on the German split https://feministberlin1968ff.de/leftist-debates/1968er-movement-splits-1969/.

33   Above n. 29, at 131. Emphases added.

student movement and nothing else, and the "newer forms of struggle" the same.

The context of the defeat of the actual political perspectives then helps to explain the curious claim in the Postone-Reinicke piece, repeated in Postone's later work, that the "Marxian critique" is fundamentally an *epistemology* which rules out any knowledge which cannot be derived out of the unfolding of the contradictions of the commodity-form. Thus:

> The Marxian dialectic presents a critical epistemology in which forms of thought are understood historically rather than as resulting from the interactions of indeterminate subjects and indeterminate objects outside of history.[34]

And

> The mature Marxian dialectic critically grasps and expresses developed bourgeois society as the first real social totality: one whose entire determinate reality can be unfolded logically from a single abstract structuring form - the commodity in its double character as a total system.[35]

These are merely quotations illustrative of a point elaborated, but not really justified, over the course of the article.

This argument is an *extension* of a point which is already written into the foundations of the Frankfurt School; right

---

34   Above n. 29, at 135.
35   Id. 136.

Michael Sommer

at the beginnings of György Lukács's *History and Class Consciousness*:

> Let us assume for the sake of argument that recent research had disproved once and for all every one of Marx's individual theses. Even if this were to be proved, every serious 'orthodox' Marxist would still be able to accept all such modern findings without reservation and hence dismiss all of Marx's theses in toto — without having to renounce his orthodoxy for a single moment. Orthodox Marxism, therefore, does not imply the uncritical acceptance of the results of Marx's investigations. It is not the 'belief' in this or that thesis, nor the exegesis of a 'sacred' book. On the contrary, orthodoxy refers exclusively to method.[36]

It is necessary to point out that this argument was already a means of intellectual closure against adverse evidence — as is, in fact, *here* transparent. The background is the influence of Max Weber on Lukács: what Lukács does is to concede the bulk of Weber's and other contemporary criticisms of Marx and Marxism, while holding onto an image of the proletariat as an imagined "revolutionary subject" which can escape the toils of Weberian industrial "rationalism."[37] What was involved was *not* the actual warts-and-all workers' movement of trade unions, coops, campaigns and

---

36 https://www.marxists.org/archive/lukacs/works/history/orthodox.htm.
37 Discussion e.g. Gareth Stedman Jones, 'The Marxism of the Early Lukács: an Evaluation' *NLR* I/70, (1971), 27-64; Zoltan Tarr, 'A Note on Weber and Lukács' *Int J Politics, Culture, and Society*, Vol. 3, (1989), 131-139.

collectivist parties, growing out of class conflict driven by capitalists' drive to increase exploitation; it was this warts-and-all movement which Marx and Engels conceived as showing the potential emancipatory role of the proletariat as pointing, *in a very approximate way*, towards the *possibility* of human cooperative activity in general. Rather, Lukács posited an imagined proletarian consciousness, achievable only by the "Leninist party," as a form of Hegelian subject in a subject-object dialectic. In the cold war period Stalinism in the east, and the apparent capture of the trade unions by the capitalist states in the west, killed this utopian image of the working class as emancipatory "knowing Subject"; hence the SDS-ers' Marcusian alternatives.[38]

The death of the SDS projects then meant that there was a need for a *further* intellectual closure against adverse evidence, going beyond that already contained in Lukács. In Postone and Reinicke, and in Postone's later work, we get additional and increasingly elaborate theorization of why the working-class movement is purely internal to capitalism — and an intellectual closure against any evidence *within Marx* which might be adverse to this interpretation.

---

38   Some useful critical perspective on this evolution in Tom Bottomore, *The Frankfurt School and its Critics*, 2nd edition, (Routledge, 2002); also Stuart Jeffries, *Grand Hotel Abyss* (Verso, 2016).

Michael Sommer

Even if the SDS projects are now dead as a dodo, Postone and Reinicke tell us, we are *still* to cling to Marcusian "Marxian" thought against the substantial evidence for "traditional Marxism." But whence is an emancipatory project to come from in this "critical theory?" The nearest approach is in Postone's "Anti-Semitism" article:

> ... the abstract domination of capital, which — particularly with rapid industrialization — caught people up in a web of dynamic forces they could not understand, became perceived as the domination of International Jewry. This was particularly true in countries such as Germany, in which the development of industrial capitalism was not only very rapid, but occurred in the absence of a previous bourgeois revolution and its consequent hegemonic liberal values and political culture.[39]

Here "bourgeois revolution" must mean the *American* revolution, given the difficulties of analysis of the English revolution and the extensive French complicity in the Holocaust. And "hegemonic liberal values and political culture" — again an appeal to the USA, given the weight of Conservatism in British politics — is to be understood as the essential prophylactic against antisemitism as "fore-shortened anticapitalism."[40]

---

39   Above n. 29, 107.
40   Postone's 1985 "Review: Jean Cohen on Marxian Critical Theory," *Theory and Society*, Vol. 14, 233-246, makes the point that liberalism is essential more explicit.

The fall of the Soviet bloc, and the brief ascendancy of ideas that history had come to an end in liberalism, and so on,[41] renewed the plausibility of this sort of reasoning. Thus, for example, Postone's adherents in the Platypus Affiliated Society.[42] But class has again returned — this time not in the form of working class mass actions, as in the late 1960s to 1970s, but in the restoration of the "reserve army of labor" and intensifying exploitation of increasingly precarious labor, returning us to "19th century" conditions. And liberalism tied to this project of intensified exploitation has in consequence issued in growing nationalism and illiberalism in politics world-wide. This side of the coin ideologically reflects the aspect of *personal* domination in capitalism, which is in fact as prominent in Marx as capitalism as freedom and impersonal rules, but which Postone attempted to exclude from "Marxian" analysis by his intellectual closure in the definition of the dialectic.

This intellectual closure, then takes us back to the beginning: the severe deficiencies of the argument of the "Anti-Semitism" article, and those of its followers, which

---

41   Francis Fukuyama, "The End of History?" *The National Interest*, No. 16 (1989), pp. 3-18 is only the most celebrated such product.

42   E.g., Chris Cutrone, "Lenin's Liberalism" (2011) https://platypus1917.org/2011/06/01/lenins-liberalism/.

are closed against both evidence and alternative analyses. Michael Sommer has exposed these deficiencies for us in the article translated here.

— Mike Macnair

ANTI-POSTONE

WRONG, BUT EFFECTIVE

"Break the rule of banks and corporations," the protesters chanted, while others tore at the police cordons erected outside the European Central Bank tower in Frankfurt. Despite the massive presence of state forces, more than 3,000 people attended the Blockupy protests against European Union crisis policies in late May 2013. Their objective was to "deliver resistance against the government and the European troika's austerity policies [...] to one of the centers of the European crisis regime: the headquarters of the European Central Bank and many German banks and corporations, which are the profiteers of these policies."[1] Despite severe police violence, the organizers deemed the protests a success, emphasizing that "resistance against the crisis policies, their social effects [...] and resistance to the

---

1   "Blockupy Frankfurt! Widerstand im Herzen des europäi-
        schen Krisenregimes," at http://blockupy.org/2091/sie-wol-
        len-kapitalismus-ohne-demokratie-wir-wollen-demokratie-
        ohne-kapitalismus/

infringement of democratic rights are inseparable. They want capitalism without democracy, we want democracy without capitalism."[2]

Meanwhile in Hamburg, some felt rather differently about what was occurring in Frankfurt. The local radio station Freies Sender Kombinat (FSK) hosted a panel debate dedicated to the imminent protests. "Finance capital," it was said, was seen by Blockupy activists as a synonym for "wicked" capital. The anti-bank critics, one of the panelists argued, were all in agreement that "the money lender — i.e. the pawnbroker, the banker confronting ordinary craftsmen and honest workers who build the industry and represent the concrete" is the "enemy of all that is decent." And he was certain that the Frankfurt protesters would not leave it at that: "The wicked banker, the wicked money lender, and ultimately the wicked Jew who embodies all these things — that's what it always boils down to in the end." On May 1st 2013, he continued, neo-Nazis had likewise shown up in Frankfurt to demonstrate against the crisis. This, he said, just showed that one could not be "disdainful enough of the German left."

---

2   "Sie wollen Kapitalismus ohne Demokratie, wir wollen Demokratie ohne Kapitalismus," see Linksjugend Solid website at https://www.linksjugend-solid.de/sie-wollen-kapitalismus-ohne-demokratie-wir-wollen-demokratie-ohne-kapitalismus/.

Are human chains outside the European Central Bank and Deutsche Bank a modern version of the Nazi campaign "Don't buy from Jews!"? Are Blockupy activists the new brownshirts? Not unjustifiably, some might find these notions perplexing. Others merely shake their heads in silence — they have heard their fair share of similar accusations by now. And indeed, hardly any social protest has not faced charges of antisemitism or Nazism in recent years. This was true for the so-called Monday demonstrations against welfare cuts and the G8 protests in Heiligendamm — and now, Blockupy is targeted too.

If we take a closer look at the denunciations, two things become apparent. Firstly, the attacks — which are often presented with an air of utmost scientificity — are regularly carried out in the name of anti-fascism. Secondly, they always follow the same pattern. The protesters and activists, it is claimed, criticize "intangible capital," while at the same time "hypostatizing labor" and contrasting "cunning locusts" with "honest workers." Two terms invariably mark the poles of the asserted dichotomy: "abstract" and "concrete." Circulation is abstract, whereas production is concrete. Money is abstract, while labor is concrete. And so on.

Nine times out of ten, the footnote appendices of the relevant articles and leaflets contain references to a text by

Moishe Postone that was originally published as early as 1979: "Anti-Semitism and National Socialism." In but a few pages, Postone's argument — embedded in reflections on the public reception of the TV miniseries *Holocaust* [first aired in West Germany in January 1979 — Translator] — places "modern anti-Semitism" at the center of the analysis of German fascism, construes it as hatred of the "abstract value dimension" of capitalist society falsely personified in "the Jew," and consequently interprets it as the revolt of a "foreshortened anti-capitalism."[3]

Postone's essay, which was later frequently revised by its author and reprinted many times, has enjoyed immense popularity and wide circulation especially since the nineties.[4] It is hard to keep track of the number of times it has

---

3   The German equivalent, *verkürzter Antikapitalismus*, is far more commonly used in Germany and Austria than its English equivalents are heard in the English-speaking world. When the term appears in English texts, it is often translated from German as 'truncated' or 'abridged' anti-capitalism — Translator.

4   For an edit history, see Postone 2005, p. 214. Where possible, we will refer to the most widely known English version of Postone's text, available from the *Anarchist Library* and *Libcom* websites — see Postone 1986 in the bibliography. In some cases — i.e., when the author cites sections that only appear in the original 1979 version of "National Socialism and Anti-Semitism" — we will refer to that version, which is accessible in multiple formats at the *Internet Archive*. In these instances, our page numbers will refer to the PDF version at https://ia802801.us.archive.org/23/items/AntiSemitis-mAndNationalSocialismMoishePostone/Anti-Semitism%20and%20National%20Socialism%20-%20Moishe%20Postone.pdf.

appeared on antifa websites, and its theses are widespread in the [German] antifa movement. In the 2011 published volume, titled *Antifa — Geschichte und Organisierung (Antifa — History and Organization)*, the authors conclude that in the nineties the "orthodox left conception of capitalism was modernized with elements of critical theory." According to them, one clear demonstration of this is that theories of fascism now place antisemitism at the "center of their explanatory approaches." In the course of this transformation, they continue, anti-fascists have generally accepted that "society does not work in such a way that ruling elites sit down together and plan world history." Instead, concepts such as "internal dynamics" and "factual constraints" came into focus.[5] What the authors describe as a "modernization" of contemporary social theory is, not least, the history of the reception of Postone's theses originally advanced in "Anti-Semitism and National Socialism." The notion that capitalism is "abstract power," or that it has an "abstract side," is taken for granted by many anti-fascists across the various factions of the German antifa spectrum today.[6] The same is true for the assertion

---

5   Keller, Kögler, Krawinkel and Schlemermeyer 2011, p. 98 and 139.

6   See overview in Keller, Kögler, Krawinkel and Schlemermeyer 2011, p. 126.

that fascism — or antisemitism, for hardly any distinction is made between the two — is essentially a "hatred" for the "abstract" and an affirmation of the "concrete."

For example, "chopping wood"

This conceptual couplet, abstract vs. concrete, has since taken on a life of its own. As an interpretive model, it is considered almost self-explanatory, not requiring any further discussion. Deferentially, the underlying arguments are described as "just about the most strenuous mental contortions hitherto demanded of left-wing thinking" — after all, they deal with "commodity and value form; fetish critique and money theory; Hegel, Marx and Lukács."[7] Almost as if it were a self-evident fact, one paper states that "the [Nazis'] objective was to annihilate the counter-principle to their own utopia by annihilating the Jews — namely circulation, abstraction, liberalism, and Bolshevism."[8] Fair enough — who hasn't heard of "abstraction?" And so, the author considers it sufficient to cryptically refer to the alter-globalization movement as a "transnational

---

7   'Linker Zahnschmerz. Der Streit um Israel könnte eine theo-
     retische Selbstbesinnung unter Teilbereichslinken einleiten'
     — accessible in Anti Atom Aktuell archives via Wayback
     Machine: https://web.archive.org/web/20120610132526/
     http://www.anti-atom-aktuell.de/.
8   Weiß 2005, p. 3.

movement for the liberation of value from abstraction"[9] in order to label it "antisemitic" and associate it with fascism.

Entire word clusters have since been assigned to this conceptual couplet, making political categorization easier when in doubt. Alongside the stock market, intellectualism and the artificial, a long list of concepts is considered "abstract" — for instance, idleness, luxury, debauchery, freedom of movement, migration from the countryside to the cities and lust. In contrast, all that might strike common sense as "concrete" is subsumed into the corresponding category: "warmth and security" [*Nestwärme*],[10] " chopping wood,"[11] "prole romanticism" and "*Altbier* [a traditionally brewed beer from Düsseldorf] "[12] have long been adopted as synonyms for "Nazi" in the relevant debates.[13]

---

9   Autonome Antifa Nordost Berlin (AANO): 'Die unendlichen Geschichten des Robert Kurz' at https://www.nadir.org/nadir/initiativ/aanb/phase2.html.
10 Mario Möller: 'Gemeinschaft über alles' in *Jungle World* 1 March 2012, available at https://jungle.world/artikel/2012/09/gemeinschaft-ueber-alles.
11 Bundesarbeitskreis Shalom: 'Warum Solidarität mit Israel?' at http://bak-shalom.de/index.php/bildung/warum-solidaritat-mit-israel/.
12 Alex Feuerherdt: 'Was für Eltern muss man haben... ', accessible via Wayback Machine: https://web.archive.org/web/20140327023132/prodomo-online.org/ausgabe-1/archiv/artikel/n/was-fuer-eltern-muss-man-haben.html
13 As has been reported to me more recently, wholemeal bread and buying from organic farmers have also come under suspicion of 'hypostatizing the concrete', and flat shares have been dissolved in the wake of heated debates over the question of whether communal living was 'Nazi' or not.

Although Postone's text was criticized from early on, the theses advanced in "Anti-Semitism and National Socialism" have truly gone places.[14] Much has been said on the subject since, while this has hardly diminished the popularity of the text. What is more, its critics have barely touched upon the "antinomy between the concrete and the abstract" that supposedly permeates capitalist relations and as a conceptual twosome provides a reference point even for the most absurd charges of antisemitism and Nazism. Yet according to the Postone critic Gerhard Hanloser, it is precisely this asserted antinomy that identifies Postone as the "founding father of subjectless Marxism" in antisemitism theory as well. This alleged antinomy is also what renders his theses wrong. It will therefore be the focus of our assessment.[15]

First, we will briefly introduce the crucial sections in Postone's text. We will critically examine his reflections on Marx's analysis of the essence and appearance of the

---

14   See Enderwitz 1993; Hanloser 2011 and 2004; and Daniel Rapoport: "Wie Moishe Postone sich irrte," first part accessible via Wayback Machine at https://web.archive.org/web/20160607012633/http://www.rapoport.de/index/107/. Detlev Claussen also makes some critical remarks in Claussen 2003, p. 245.

15   Our focus is the reception and function of the text in the context of an 'anti-fascism' that targets social protest. For the historical context in which Postone's essay emerged, see Hanloser 2004.

capitalist mode of production. It will become apparent that Postone's conclusions are based on a questionable method of "free association of concepts."[16] Postone provides no adequate theory of the "essence and appearance" of capitalist society or of antisemitism. As we will see, he instead provides the blueprint for a certain type of uncritical critique. This critique presents itself with the gesture of a theoretically upgraded anti-fascism, yet in reality pursues very little apart from accusing those of fascism who defend themselves against the ravages of capitalism today.

"Abstractness, intangibility, universality, mobility"

The starting point for Postone's analysis is his observation that antisemitism, while directing its aggressions against various phenomena of modern capitalist society, has remained "conspicuously silent" on industrial capital and

---

16   In the rather literal translation of Marx's 'Notes on Adolph's Wagner's *Lehrbuch der politischen Ökonomie*' available at Marxists.org, Marx's expression *Begriffanknüpfungs-Methode*, which he used with reference to the professorial socialists, is translated as 'association-of-concepts method': "Therefore our *vir obscurus* too, who has not even noticed that my *analytic* method, which does not proceed from *man* but from a given economic period of society, has nothing in common with the German-professorial association-of-concepts method ('words are excellent for fighting with, with words a system may be built')..." — See Marx 1881. We believe that our translation 'free association of concepts' is more adequate — Translator.

10

modern technology.[17] Postone argues that, in order to explain this phenomenon and the corresponding "patterns of social critique and affirmation," the nature of the power attributed to Jews is of key importance: it is characterized by its "mysterious intangibility," its "abstract" and "universal" qualities. It is conceived as "not bound concretely," "not 'rooted'; it is deemed to be "of staggering immensity," "difficult to check" and "hidden — conspiratorial."[18] Moreover, it is "considered to be a form of power that does not manifest itself directly, but must find another mode of expression. It seeks a concrete carrier..."[19] The power thus described, Postone continues, is graphically portrayed in an antisemitic poster, which shows "Germany — represented as a strong, honest worker — threatened in the West by a fat, plutocratic John Bull and in the East by a brutal, barbaric Bolshevik Commissar. Yet, these two hostile forces are mere puppets. Peering over the edge of the globe, with the puppet strings firmly in his hands, is the Jew."[20] In the antisemitic imagination, the Jew stands behind all forces that brought about the decline of traditional society at the end of the nineteenth century.

---

17   Postone 1986.
18   *Ibid.*
19   *Ibid.*
20   *Ibid.*

In these characteristics of "power attributed to the Jews," Postone recognizes precisely those traits that, for him, distinguish the "value dimension" of capitalism "in its immediacy" as described by Marx:

> When one examines the specific characteristics of the power attributed to the Jews by modern anti-Semitism — abstractness, intangibility, universality, mobility — it is striking that they are all characteristics of the value dimension of the social forms analyzed by Marx. Moreover, this dimension, like the supposed power of the Jews, does not appear as such, but always in the form of a material carrier, the commodity.[21]

From these supposedly shared characteristics, Postone concludes that the hatred of Jews is really a hatred of the "abstract" "value dimension" of capitalism — according to him, it is precisely this abstract "value dimension" that does not manifest itself in industry and technology — transferred onto a group of people. The Jews have lent themselves to this "concretization of the abstract" because, as citizens of different nations, they are the ultimate embodiment of the "abstract" citizen, as opposed to the "concrete" private person. According to Postone, the "abstract domination of capital" caught "people" up in a "web of dynamic forces they could not

---

21   Postone 1986.

understand," which therefore came to be perceived as "International Jewry." For Postone, this "abstract domination" is represented in money, in capital as an abstract "pure process," in commercial and finance capital, in the liberal state, in jurisdiction, in technocratic domination, in abstract, universal "law" and in abstract reason. Elsewhere, he summarized briefly: "The abstract domination of capitalism is personified as the Jews. Antisemitism is a revolt against global capital, misrecognized as the Jews."[22] Postone's observations culminate in his assertion that Auschwitz was the practical implementation of this "hatred of the abstract," effectively a "factory to 'destroy value.'"[23]

Ostensibly, then, two points are understood: the rule of capital is "abstract," and antisemitism is a revolt against this "abstract" — while subjectively sincere, it is necessarily misdirected against a "concrete." For Postone, the key to this insight is Marx's conception of fetishism. This theory, he writes, allows us to differentiate various perceptions of modern society in order to explain different reactions to aspects of this society (i.e., Postone's "patterns of social critique and affirmation").

---

22   Thomas 2010.
23   Postone 1986.

The "opposition between the concrete and the abstract"

Postone explains his understanding of fetishism with reference to the most basic form of this phenomenon, namely commodity fetishism, as elaborated by Marx in the first chapter of his main work, *Capital, Volume I*. After some vague — and confusing — remarks about Marx's analysis of capitalist relations, Postone writes:

> The dialectical tension between value and use-value in the commodity form requires that this "double character" be materially externalized. It appears "doubled" as money (the manifest form of value) and as the commodity (the manifest form of use-value). Although the commodity is a social form expressing both value and use-value, the effect of this externalization is that the commodity appears only as its use-value dimension, as purely material and "thingly." Money, on the other hand, then appears as the sole repository of value, as the manifestation of the purely abstract, rather than as the externalized manifest form of the value dimension of the commodity itself. The form of materialized social relations specific to capitalism appears on this level of the analysis as the opposition between money, as abstract, and "thingly" nature.[24]

However, the abstract dimension appears as "natural" in the form of "'objective', natural laws," i.e., as a "quasi-natural antinomy." For Postone, this "antinomy of the abstract and

---

24   Postone 1986.

concrete dimensions" through which social relations "present themselves" continues at the level of more complex social relations:

> The capital form, like the commodity form, is characterized by the antinomic relation of concrete and abstract, both of which appear as natural... Capital, according to Marx, is self-valorizing value. It is characterized by a continuous, ceaseless process of the self-expansion of value. This process underlies rapid, large-scale cycles of production and consumption, creation and destruction. Capital has no fixed, final form, but appears at different stages of its spiraling path in the form of money and in the form of commodities. As self-valorizing value, capital appears as pure process.[25]

For Postone, the general rule is: "Capitalist social relations appear to find their expression only in the abstract dimension."[26]

Postone thus assumes a "value dimension in its immediacy" that really exists in socio-economic reality and is characterized by "abstractness, intangibility, universality, mobility."[27] It supposedly manifests itself in concrete forms that appear "natural," yet does not lose its "abstractness." Finally, it enters people's consciousness in a manner that makes it a potential source and point of entry for narratives which ascribe social developments to a Jewish power that is "difficult to check."

---

25   Postone 1986.
26   *Ibid.*
27   *Ibid.*

To answer what all this has to do with Marx's theory of fetishism, a more detailed examination of Marx's analysis of capitalism is necessary, which we can only undertake in a cursory fashion. Even so, our assessment will hopefully make the debate easier to understand and liberate it from the pretense of being some kind of "intellectual high bar" best left to those who possess the relevant skills. It will become apparent that the "abstract value dimension" is in fact an amalgam of individual aspects of Marx's analysis taken out of context, on the one hand, and methodologically conditioned descriptions of this analysis on the other. This amalgam fails to do justice to the economic and social realities of capitalism.

From the abstract to the concrete

In order to reveal the "law of motion of modern society," Marx subjects the totality of the relations that constitute our society to a detailed analysis.[28] In *Capital*, he begins with the most basic social relations, then moves on to more complex relations step by step. His analysis thus begins with the circulation of commodities (the "market"), proceeds to production and then returns to circulation. Marx explains individual commodities and money, then moves on to complex forms, such as interest and rent. The order in which the

---

28   Marx 1990, p. 92.

different areas are presented is "determined by their mutual relation in modern bourgeois society." Marx refers to this method as "rising from the abstract to the concrete," defined as follows: "The concrete is concrete because it is the concentration of many determinations, hence unity of the diverse."[29] He uses the term in the sense of "composite" or "grown together." The full-fledged concrete is therefore society in its entirety, i.e., the real subject of analysis.

By *abstract*, on the other hand, Marx means the individual elements and partial areas of the concrete that are exposed in the process of thinking. He uses the term in the sense of the Latin word *abs-trahere*, which translates as something like "to remove from." Marx himself emphasizes this when he writes, for instance: "If we consider this in the abstract, i.e. disregarding circumstances..."[30] While in the natural sciences we can make use of the microscope and chemical reagents to expose the smallest elements, in the social sciences "the force of abstraction must replace both."[31] When rising from the abstract to the concrete, the "abstract determinations lead towards a reproduction of the concrete by way of thought."[32]

---

29   Marx 1857, chapter 1.
30   Marx 1990, p. 260.
31   Marx 1990, p. 90.
32   Marx 1857, chapter 1.

The "simplest concrete element of economics" with which Marx begins his depiction of the circulation of commodities and thus his explanation of money is the individual commodity. To examine it, one must "exclude all relations which have nothing to do with the particular object of the analysis."[33] That is to say, one must *abstract* from them — especially from money, which is yet to be explained.

The commodity is at the same time *concrete* because it is a combination of several determinations: It is both use-value and value — not just a particular piece of natural substance adapted to suit human needs, but also a product of human labor that stands in relation to other products of labor. This is owed to the fact that within the capitalist mode of production, the "social relations between individuals in the performance of their labour" are not established directly, but materially mediated "after the work is done" through the exchange of the products of labor.[34] The labors performed acquire their immediate social form in the characteristic in which they relate to other labors in the form of their products: i.e., as products not of this or that specific act of labor, but of human labor in general — abstract human labor, as Marx calls it. The commodity is the carrier of value insofar as it is not only the product of

33   Marx 1881.
34   Marx 1990, p. 171.

human labor *per se*, but, in this characteristic, stands in relation to other products of labor that possess the same characteristic.

In order to mentally capture the individual commodity as value, Marx must resort to abstraction again. Fully aware that the commodity has value only in exchange, he must think away any other commodity to which it could relate, yet without thinking away the fact of the relationship itself. This is because the value of an individual commodity exists only for the scientific observer: "A product of labor, considered in isolation, is not [...] a commodity."[35] Marx, however, isolates and fixes his gaze on the commodity before illuminating its objectivity [*Gegenständlichkeit*] as labor product and value in two steps. The value of the individual commodity and its objectivity thus become something that is difficult to put into words.

The commodity: "Impossible to grasp as a thing possessing value"

"Let us now look at the residue of the products of labour. There is nothing left of them in each case but the same phantom-like objectivity."[36] In this section of *Capital, Vol-*

---

35   Michael Heinrich, *An Introduction to the Three Volumes of Karl Marx's "Capital,"* trans. Alex Locascio (New York: Monthly Review Press, 2012), p. 53. The original German quote from Marx is: "Ein Arbeitsprodukt, für sich isoliert betrachtet, ist [also] nicht Wert [so wenig es Waare ist]" — see Marx 1987, p. 31.

36   Marx 1990, p. 128.

ume I, Marx used the terms "phantom-like objectivity" and "congealed quantities" to convey that he is describing a general property tied to the sensuous objectivity of the product of labor, but not identical with it. This general property is abstract because with respect to it, all other properties of the thing are abstracted from.

It goes without saying that the attempt to capture this characteristic poses difficulties with regard to language. In order to grasp a thing "as a merely corporeal expression of human labour," Marx writes when describing this problem, one has to "abstract from all that which makes it to be really a thing. Any objectivity of human labour which is itself abstract (i.e., without any additional quality and content) is necessarily an abstract objectivity — a *thing of thought*. In that fashion, a web of flax turns into a chimera."[37] Insofar as Marx fixes his gaze on the commodity as a product of labor, he also dubs it a "crystal" and "purely fantastic objectivity."[38] Marx's efforts to find an adequate expression are not made any easier by the fact that the commodity in this general characteristic stands in relation to other commodities, and that this characteristic thereby acquires a meaning which it does not have outside this

---

37   Marx 1867a.
38   Marx 1987, p. 32.

relation. He therefore uses some vivid metaphors: "The objectivity of commodities as values differs from Dame Quickly in the sense that 'a man knows not where to have it' [...] We may twist and turn a single commodity as we wish; it remains impossible to grasp it as a thing possessing value" — elsewhere, Marx calls it "invisible," and again he speaks of "phantom-like objectivity."[39]

Postone takes up these essentially wrong but methodologically necessary descriptions of value and its bearer[40] and interprets them as adequate descriptions — as "characteristics of the value dimension" — when he speaks of the "quality of abstractness" of the "value dimension in its immediacy."[41] However, these descriptions must not be

---

39   Marx 1990, p. 138, 128. Marx 1987, p. 7. In Shakespeare's *King Henry IV* (part 1, act III, scene III), the hostess says, "Thou art an unjust man in saying so: thou or any man knows where to have me, thou knave, thou!" Detlev Claussen uses this Shakespearean joke as a starting point for some reflections on antisemitism that are evidently based on Potstone's work: "Value appears in things and yet is not tangible anywhere: the objectivity of commodities as values differs from Dame Quickly in the sense that 'a man knows not where to have it'. Commodity owners identify this intangibility of value with the former agents of exchange, the Jews, who are also intangible and everywhere." [our translation] — Claussen 1988, p. 37.

40   See also Dieter Wolf: "Zur Methode in Marx' *Kapital* unter besonderer Berücksichtigung ihres logisch-systematischen Characters" ("On Marx's method in *Capital* with special consideration of its logical-systematic character"), PDF available from Dieter Wolf's website at http://www.dieterwolf.net/pdf/Methodenstreit_Haug_Heinrich.pdf.

41   See Postone 1986. More than a few other Marx interpreters do likewise, albeit with a different objective in mind. On

confused with what is going on in *actual social relations*. In *Capital*, any abstractions initially made are gradually withdrawn as Marx further ascends from the abstract to the concrete — all corresponding descriptions thereby lose their meaning. In social reality, there is no really existing value that is distinct from the value-form and exists in and of itself, in an "abstract" and "intangible" fashion, unmediated, as "intangible value abstraction" (peering over the edge of the market stall like "the Jew peers over the edge of the globe") and is then "materially externalized in the value-form."[42]

At the beginning of *Capital*, "coat and linen as values, each for itself, [are] reduced purely to the objectification of labor. But this reduction 'forgets' that neither of them possesses such value-objectivity [*Wertgegenständlichkeit*] on its own. They possess it only insofar as that is their common objectivity [*Gegenständlichkeit*]."[43] Marx must there-

---

the problem of the deceptive evidence of Marx's metaphors, see Dieter Wolf, "Fehlinterpretationen Vorschub leistende Mängel in Marx' Darstellung im *Kapital* und wie Marx sie hätte vermeiden können" ("Deficiencies in Marx's presentation in *Capital* that are conducive to misinterpretation, and how Marx could have avoided them"), available from Dieter Wolf's website at https://dieterwolf.net/wordpress/wp-content/uploads/2018/12/Kapital_Marx_Versaeumnisse_vermeiden.pdf.

42 See Postone 1979, p. 9.
43 Our translation — Marx 2018, p. 192. Original German text: "So wurden der Rock und Leinwand als Werte, jedes für sich, auf Vergegenständlichung menschlicher Arbeit schlechthin

fore return to this relation to other commodities (not for-
gotten, of course, but deliberately abstracted from) before
he goes on to explain money and more complex relations:

> However, let us remember that commodities possess an
> objective character as values only in so far as they are all
> expressions of an identical social substance, human labour,
> that their objective character as values is therefore purely
> social. From this it follows self-evidently that it can only
> appear in the social relation between commodity and com-
> modity. In fact we started from exchange-value, or the ex-
> change relation of commodities, in order to track down the
> value that lay hidden within it. We must now return to this
> form of appearance of value.[44]

— i.e., we must ultimately return to the relation between priced commodities and money.

Mystical money, abstract capital

Of course, it is not Marx's analysis that generates money,
but the "social act" of the commodity owners.[45] Their be-

---

reduziert. Aber in dieser Reduktion wurde vergessen, daß
keines für sich solche Wertgegenständlichkeit ist, sondern
daß sie solches nur sind, soweit das ihnen gemeinsame Gegenständlichkeit ist."

44   Marx 1990, pp. 138–9.
45   Marx 2015 [1887], p. 61. Here, the original, Engels-edited
      Moor/ Aveling translation of the relevant section in *Capital,
      Vol. I* ("But only the *action of society* can turn a particular com-
      modity into the universal equivalent" — Marx 1990, p. 180,
      my emphasis) seems more appropriate than the Ben Fowkes
      translation for Penguin Books ("But a particular commodi-
      ty cannot become the universal equivalent except by a *social
      act*," my emphasis) — Translator.

havior in the "market" produces and reproduces anew the relation between commodity and money every day. What Marx relates about the underlying relations of commodities as products of labor in his account is not known to the commodity owners. All they can possibly know about the value of individual commodities which appears in money is based on what they know about money in the first place. It is only now that we can answer the question as to how value appears to the people involved. The question is, then, "what do people know of exchange-value, given that value is not intrinsically factual to them?"[46]

The use-value of the money commodity, as a commodity historically fixed in its function as a universal equivalent, acquires its meaning of immediate exchangeability with any other commodity through its relation to other commodities. Why this happens, the "market participants" do not realize. They are unaware that in concretely useful labor, which produces the exchange-value of the equivalent commodity, the "sensibly-concrete counts as the mere form of appearance or definite form of realisation of the ab-

---

46   Our translation. See Wolf, Dieter: 'Kommentare zu dem Beitrag von Michael Jäger im Blog der Zeitschrift *Der Freitag*: „Die andere Gesellschaft (48): „Von Adorno zu Luhmann"', PDF available from Dieter Wolf's website at https://dieter-wolf.net/wordpress/wp-content/uploads/2018/12/Wert_Wertform_Geld_Replik_2_Jaeger_1_2_.pdf.

stractly general," namely, of the characteristic of all other labor of being human labor at all.[47] That is because:

> What appears to happen is not that a particular commodity becomes money because all other commodities express their values in it, but, on the contrary, that all other commodities universally express their values in a particular commodity because it is money. The movement through which this process has been mediated vanishes in its own result, leaving no trace behind.[48]

Marx refers to the exchangeability of money, which is intrinsically factual but not immediately explicable to everyday consciousness, as its "mystical" character: he speaks of a "mystery of commodities."[49] Alongside the "intangibility" of value, this provides another reference point for Postone's description of the characteristics of the value dimension: "mysterious intangibility, abstractness." However, Marx does not resume here the previously mentally captured "abstractness" of value, as Postone suggests when referring to money as the "manifestation of the purely abstract." Rather, he describes a characteristic of money whose origin in social relations is not apparent in the money itself — a property that one might roughly describe as "not directly explicable social function of immediate ex-

---

47   Marx 1867b.
48   Marx 1990, p. 187.
49   Marx 1990, p. 169.

changeability."[50] In this sense, it is also possible to say that money is universal. The fact that Postone lumps this term together with "abstractness" and "intangibility," however, suggests that his approach is borne less by an effort to understand capitalist social forms than by a pursuit of inferences by analogy.

Marx discusses two ways in which the "mystical character" of money, its immediate exchangeability, can be explained without recourse to the underlying process — that is, "fetishistically." Firstly, the immediate exchangeability of money can be attributed, in a crude materialist fashion, as a natural property. Just as "being heavy"[51] is its natural property, it then appears that money is "endowed with the form of value by nature itself."[52] The second way to explain its direct exchangeability is to pass it off, in an equally crude idealist fashion, as a result of social arrangements, as a deliberate simplification of exchange — money as a "cunningly devised aid" [*pfiffig ausgedachtes Auskunftsmittel*].[53]

---

50   Postone 1986.
51   Marx 1990, p. 149.
52   *Ibid.*
53   Our translation — In the German vocabulary of the eighteenth and nineteenth centuries, the word *Auskunfsmittel* meant tool, means, aid, recourse. The original English translation of the relevant sentence reads: "On the other hand, they then persistently regard barter as a form well adapted to commodity exchange, suffering merely from certain technical inconveniences, to overcome which money has been cunningly devised." — Marx 1859, chapter 1. Translator.

Michael Sommer

Postone does not even take notice of this ambiguity, this core of all ideological — i.e., false — conceptions of our society, when he one-sidedly proclaims that "the abstract" appears to be "quasi-natural" and that abstract and concrete "both" appear to be "natural."[54] Moreover — in sharp contrast to the importance Postone attaches to the difference between essence and appearance — it is not at all clear why, and especially how, the "quality of abstractness" appears in social reality and enters people's consciousness. For him, "fetishization" consists in the "concretization of the abstract" — that is to say, in making tangible what is in itself intangible. Thus, the quest to comprehend social forms and their relation to (ideological) modes of thinking that drove Marx evaporates into the trivial suggestion that that which is not instantly comprehensible are probably forms of value.

Postone then continues his questionable methodological approach of picking up methodologically conditioned terms and treating them as adequate descriptions of the matter at hand when he writes: "The capital form, like the commodity form, is characterized by the antinomic relation of concrete and abstract, both of which appear to be natural." The antinomy now supposedly consists in the fact that the "double character (labor process and

---

54   Postone 1986.

valorization process) allows industrial production to appear as a purely material, creative process, separable from capital."[55]

Here, Postone's strange imprecision with regard to essence and appearance rears its head again: capital "has no fixed, final form, but appears at different stages of its spiraling path in the form of money and in the form of commodities [...] Capital appears as pure process."[56] Well, which one is it, one wants to ask? All the more so since Postone continues: "Capital itself — or what is understood as the negative aspect of capitalism — is understood only in terms of the manifest form of its abstract dimension: finance and interest capital"[57] However, in fact it is precisely there that it does not appear as an "abstract process,"[58] but as the "ability of money or a commodity to valorize its own value independent of reproduction." Marx calls this "the capital mystification in the most flagrant form."[59]

Postone's readers do not learn what creates the impression that capital has the capacity to multiply not in the process of production, but outside that process as lendable money, as a thing — i.e., Postone does not tell us what

---

55   Postone 1986.
56   *Ibid.*
57   *Ibid.*
58   See Marx 1992, p. 185.
59   Marx 1991, p. 516.

"objective fact" this notion is based on (a fact which Marx describes in the following words:

> "Talk about centralization! The credit system, which has its focal point in the allegedly national banks and the big money-lenders and usurers that surround them, is one enormous centralization and gives this class of parasites a fabulous power not only to decimate the industrial capitalists periodically but also to interfere in actual production in the most dangerous manner — and this crew know nothing of production and have nothing at all to do with it.").[60]

Nor does he tell us anything about the real subsumption of labor under capital and why, in the form of domination of dead labor over living labor, it goes hand in hand with the transformation of the labor process according to the conditions of the valorization of value, through which labor indeed becomes more abstract.

Thus, without further examining the social relations in which the capital relation is reproduced and concealed by the actions of human beings, Postone summarily resumes the terminology from the first pages of *Capital*: according to him, capital appears in its "abstract dimension" — it appears as an "abstract process." This is supposed to tell us all we need to know,[61] and one is reminded of Frederick

---

60   Marx 1991, p. 678–9.
61   Daniel Rapoport rightly notes: "How quickly he [Postone] infers from the double character of the commodity to that of the entire wealth of appearances — or rather: poverty of

Engels: "First the concept of the object is fabricated from the object; then the spit is turned round, and the object is measured by its reflexion, the concept. The object is then to conform to the concept, not the concept to the object."[62]

Postone elaborates the conclusion to this evolution from the "abstract dimension" to the "abstract domination" of capital in his book *Time, Labor, and Social Domination*. The social relations of capital, he writes, "exist not as overt interpersonal relations but as a quasi-independent set of structures that are opposed to individuals."[63] He illustrates this idea with the following quote from Marx: "These objective dependency relations also appear,... in such a way that individuals are now ruled by abstractions, whereas earlier they depended on one another." Postone comments: "Capitalism is a system of abstract, impersonal domination."[64]

Apparently, this abstract "quasi-independent set of structures" has the capacity to become "even more abstract" — namely, in the transition from Fordist to post-Fordist capitalism.[65] And, with so much abstractness

---

appearances — of capitalism is surprising" (our translation) — Daniel Rapoport: "Wie Moishe Postone sich irrte," first part accessible via Wayback Machine at https://web.archive. org/web/20160607012633/http://www.rapoport.de/in- dex/107/.

62   Engels 1894, p. 59.
63   Postone 1993, p. 139.
64   *Ibid*.
65   Postone 2006, p. 107.

going on, there isn't even any talk of the "abstract" appearing in a concrete carrier anymore — all that remains is the notion of a purely subjective "concretization of the abstract," "a fetishized identification of the United States with global capital," or a "tendency to grasp the abstract... as concrete," etc. The "quality of the abstract" is perfect, the "manifestation of the purely abstract" is now but a notional (mis)conception held by "people."

Following Marx, one can indeed "speak of a reversal of subject and object insofar as everything that is decisive for the sociality of labor, from the commodity — or from the most basic forms of value — to developed forms of capital, plays out on the side of the object, i.e., in the social relation of things confronting the subjects."[66]

Yet while Postone implies that the forms of value develop, as it were, from abstract value "in itself" and take on a life of their own independently of social relations, Marx explains how the social relation of things — the relation of social labor in the form of its products — gives specific shape and specific structure to the social relations themselves.

He describes how and why the most basic economic relations that he depicted in the beginning are, "conceived

---

66   Our translation — Wolf 2007, p. 3.

by themselves, [...] pure abstractions; but these relations are, in reality, mediated by the deepest antithesis."[67]

For him, value is, as Ulrich Enderwitz aptly notes, "a component of the world," not "a factor that is absolutely and autonomously distinct from the world or exists in opposition to it."[68] Value does not exist in an "abstract" mode or "in itself," "above and in opposition to individuals and classes."[69] It is only through the actions of people that it has, in its different forms, power over society.

"Independent powers, personified in those who own them"

Marx studied this power, the effect of objectified social relations upon societies, and how it was perceived in the course of capitalist history thoroughly. To understand it, one must always start from the consideration that if "abstract human labor, as a universal social form of concrete useful labor, has, on the one hand, negative effects on the economic-social relation," this is not because the general characteristic is abstract (like every general characteristic) [...] All negative effects, including those which result from the degradation of the labor process into a means to an end,

---

67   Marx 1857, chapter 5.
68   Our translation — Enderwitz 2005, p. 58.
69   Postone 1993, p. 140.

namely for the valorization of value, are effects that forms of value, composed of manifestations of abstract human labor, have upon economic-social contexts."[70] These value forms "live" only in the actions of humans.

In a preliminary paper to his economic works, Marx argues that it is not enough to leave it at forms of appearance alone.

> As soon as gold and silver (or any other commodity) have developed themselves as measure of value and means of circulation [...] they become money without the society's aid or desire. Their power appears as a kind of fate, and the consciousness of men, especially in social orders declining because of a deeper development of exchange-value relations, rebels against the power which a physical matter, a thing, acquires with respect to men, against the domination of the accursed metal which appears as sheer insanity. It is in money, and in its most abstract and hence most senseless, incomprehensible form, the form in which all mediation is sublated, that this transformation of social interrelations into a solid, overwhelming, individual-subsuming social relationship first appears.[71]

With the formal and actual subordination of labor to capital, society is shaken to its foundations, and "all the

---

70   Our translation — Dieter Wolf: "Bemerkungen zum Zusammenhang zwischen Wert und Kapital," p. 14. PDF available at https://dieterwolf.net/wordpress/wp-content/uploads/2019/01/Zusammenhang_Wert_Kapital.pdf. See also Dieter Wolf: 'Elmar Flatscharts "wertkritische" Auseinandersetzung mit Ingo Elbes *Kapital*— Interpretation' at https://dieterwolf.net/wordpress/wp-content/uploads/2019/12/Flatschart-Kritik-1.pdf.
71   Marx 1987b, p. 487.

corresponding old, traditional relationships of population and production, economic relationships" disintegrate as the "rather violent economic upheaval which Thomas More deplored" unfolds.[72]

But this movement does not just hang free in the air: circulation "appears independent with respect to them [the participants in the exchange, i.e., the economic structure of society — Author] as intermediary trade whose carriers, such as the Semites in the interstices of the ancient world, and the Jews, Lombards, and Normans in the interstices of the medieval society, alternately represent with respect to them the different moments of circulation — money and commodity."[73] The same is true of capital, which has already passed its historical genesis: it is the capitalist in whom capital is "endowed with consciousness and will"[74] and who, "fanatically intent on the valorization of value," "ruthlessly forces the human race to produce for production's sake."[75] "The self-valorisation of capital — the creation of surplus-value — is therefore the determining, dominating, and overmastering purpose of the capitalist, the absolute driving force and content of his action."[76] If,

---

72   Marx 1987b, p. 481.
73   *Ibid.*
74   Marx 1990, p. 255.
75   Marx 1990, p. 739.
76   Marx 1861–64.

then, the increment of value "appears, with regard to the existing sum of value or money, as its *determination* its inner driving force, its tendency" — as the "automatic subject" of the process, in Marx's words, it appears "with regard to the *capitalist* i.e. the owner of this sum of money... as his *intention*, his *purpose*."[77] Put differently, "the secret of the self-valorization of capital resolves itself into the fact that it has at its disposal a definite quantity of the unpaid labour of other people [*fremder Arbeit*]."[78] Thus "capital is indeed separable from the individual capitalist, but not from the capitalist, who as such confronts the worker,"[79] and whom "a real freemasonry vis-a-vis the working class as a whole" unites with his class companions.[80]

Money, capital, surplus-value, profit, interest, and so on are the forms of appearance by means of which economic social relations — in which value and abstract human

---

77   Marx 1861–64. To Postone devotees, on the other hand, the capitalist is only a "slave" to value and no less subject to the domination of capital than the worker. "Maybe [Deutsche Bank boss] Josef Ackermann would like to do something else in his life, too — carpentry perhaps?", is how a contributor to the website *Emanzipation oder Barberei* expressed his sympathy in 2009. (http://emanzipationoderbarbarei.blogsport. de/2009/10/06/migration-und-oekonomie/). Where Marx still scoffed at the ideology of "self-chastisement of this modern penitent of Vishnu, the capitalist" (Marx 1990, p. 745), the Postoneans are dead serious.
78   Marx 1990, p. 672.
79   Marx 1857, chapter 6.
80   Marx 1991, p. 300.

labor are general social forms — exercise their power in practice.[81] Their autonomy develops to the point of mutual personification.[82] They are not autonomous "abstract" powers, but "autonomous powers, personified in their owners."[83]

"Consolidated, nourished and inculcated by the ruling classes by all means available"

We must now return to Postone's "abstract domination" and the Marx citation he invokes to back up his thesis. Postone quotes Marx as saying: "These objective dependency relations also appear... in such a way that individuals are now ruled by abstractions, whereas earlier they depended on one another." Postone comments: "Capitalism is a system of abstract, impersonal domination."[84]

If we consult Marx's original text, we find the following reflections, which we shall reproduce at length to illustrate the difference between Marx and Postone:

---

81   See also Dieter Wolf: "Elmar Flatscharts "wertkritische" Auseinandersetzung mit Ingo Elbes *Kapital*— Interpretation" at https://dieterwolf.net/wordpress/wp-content/uploads/2019/12/Flatschart-Kritik-1.pdf.
82   Marx 1861–64.
83   Marx 1857, chapter 2a (https://www.marxists.org/archive/marx/works/1864/economic/ch02a.htm.)
84   Postone 1993, p. 139.

These *objective* dependency relations [in bourgeois society — Author] also appear, in antithesis to those of *personal* dependence (the objective dependency relation is nothing more than social relations which have become independent and now enter into opposition to the seemingly independent individuals; i.e. the reciprocal relations of production separated from and autonomous of individuals) in such a way that individuals are now ruled by *abstractions,* whereas earlier they depended on one another.[85]

Unlike Postone, however, Marx does not conceive of these "abstractions" as "abstract" forms of value. Indeed he continues as follows:

The abstraction, or idea, however, is nothing more than the theoretical expression of those material relations which are their lord and master. Relations can be expressed, of course, only in ideas, and thus philosophers have determined the reign of ideas to be the peculiarity of the new age, and have identified the creation of free individuality with the overthrow of this reign. This error was all the more easily committed, from the ideological stand-point, as this reign exercised by the relations (this objective dependency, which, incidentally, turns into certain definite relations of personal dependency, but stripped of all illusions) appears within the consciousness of individuals as the reign of ideas, and because the belief in the permanence of these ideas, i.e. of these objective relations of dependency, is of course consolidated, nourished and inculcated by the ruling classes by all means available.[86]

---

85   Marx 1857, chapter 3.
86   Marx 1857, chapter 3. Marx thus develops an idea that he
        had already expressed in a letter to P. V. Annenkov in 1846:

37

Of course, it is correct to say that capitalist society is not based on a relationship of domination and servitude premised onto the relationship of producers to their labor.

This does not mean, however, that such relations no longer exist under capitalism; rather, it means that "in the modern world, personal relations flow purely out of relations of production and exchange."[87] Postone's notion of a "rule of abstractions," on the other hand, itself turns out to be ideological.

Capital, which characterizes modern society, is identical with the existing class relations. Capital is not an "abstract process" — it is not a structure that moves independently in a mystical and irrational fashion, one-sidedly confronting social relations irrespective of the actions of human be-

---

"Thus Mr Proudhon chiefly because he doesn't know history, fails to see that, in developing his productive faculties, i.e. in living, man develops certain inter-relations, and that the nature of these relations necessarily changes with the modification and the growth of the said productive faculties. He fails to see that *economic categories* are but *abstractions* of those real relations, that they are truths only in so far as those relations continue to exist. Thus he falls into the error of bourgeois economists who regard those economic categories as eternal laws and not as historical laws which are laws only for a given historical development, a specific development of the productive forces. Thus, instead of regarding politico-economic categories as abstractions of actual social relations that are transitory and historical, Mr Proudhon, by a mystical inversion, sees in the real relations only the embodiment of those abstractions. Those abstractions are themselves formulas which have been slumbering in the bosom of God the Father since the beginning of the world." — Marx 1846.

87   Marx 1857, chapter 3.

ings. Value is only functional through its forms within the capital relation. Money, like capital, is not just "impersonal wealth." Both "put social power as a thing into the hands of the private person, who as such uses this power."[88]

"The real Shylock"

It is often suggested that Postone's theses build on the reflections of Frankfurt School critical theory. However, any interpretation of antisemitism which suggests that the abstract value dimension is "pulled into" real social relations, namely by way of a necessarily wrong identification of Jews with value, is diametrically opposed to the interpretation outlined by Max Horkheimer and Theodor W. Adorno. They viewed antisemitism more as an invalid attempt to "shunt" social domination and servitude from the structure of social relations shaped by value and its forms. In *Dialectic of Enlightenment*, Horkheimer and Adorno wrote: "[The Jew] is indeed the scapegoat, not only for individual maneuvers and machinations but in the wider sense that the economic injustice of the whole class is attributed to him."[89] Gerhard Hanloser commented on this section, "Now, one might stumble over the formulation 'injustice,' but at least here the connection is

88   Marx 1987b.
89   Horkheimer and Adorno 2002, p. 141.

made clear between exploitation, oppression, and Antisemitism as an unprecedented act of displacement by means of which 'The Jews' are offered to those 'mutilated by domination' as a quid pro quo of the suspended class struggle."[90]

For Horkheimer and Adorno, antisemitism is certainly not the result of some kind of "foreshortened" or "abridged" anti-capitalism [*verkürzter Antikapitalismus*]. From the point of view of the factory owner, they write, it is the perfect ideology that explains why he supposedly has no part in exploitation:

> The factory owner ventured and raked in like a great merchant or banker. He calculated, procured, bought, sold. In the market he competed with the merchants and bankers for the profit due to his capital. But he grabbed not merely from the market but from the source: as a functionary of the class system he took care not to go short of the fruits of his workers' labor. The workers had to deliver as much as possible. Like a true Shylock he insisted on his contract. By virtue of owning the machines and materials, he forced the others to produce. He called himself the producer, but he and everyone secretly knew the truth. The productive work of the capitalist, whether he justified his profit as the reward of enterprise, as under liberalism, or as the director's salary, as today, was the ideology which concealed the nature of the labor contract and the rapacity of the economic system in general.[91]

90   Hanloser 2011.
91   Horkheimer and Adorno 2002, p. 142.

The fact that the active capitalist can only exercise his function as a representative of the means of production is hidden behind the opposition between productive function within the reproduction process and ownership of capital outside of that process. The industrial capitalist, in contrast to the owner of money capital, "appears therefore not as functioning capital but rather as a functionary independent of capital, as a simple bearer of the labour process in general; as a worker, and a wage-worker at that,"[92] so the "labour of exploiting and the labour exploited are identical, both being labour." Because the factory owner is aware of this lie, the Frankfurtians argue, his antisemitism is the self-hatred of the parasite.

Moreover, for Adorno and Horkheimer antisemitism fuses a whole series of displacements — "the Jew" takes the place not only of the factory owner, but also of the merchant and the money lender. The common reason is the disappearance of profit, i.e., the "form of surplus-value specifically characteristic to the capitalist mode of production,"[93] from the canon of legitimate social sources of income, capital — interest; land — rent; labor — wages. This is where antisemitism, according to Horkheimer and Adorno, has its specifically economic grounds.

---

92   Marx 1991, p. 505.
93   Marx 1991, p. 953.

Postone at least takes this aspect into account when he writes that antisemitic ideology was particularly "functional for the development of industrial capitalism in crisis," and that National-Socialist ideology was "in the interests of capital."[94] To his disciples, these remarks must be completely incomprehensible. They already seemed strangely out of place in Postone's original text, which is probably why they were omitted from subsequent versions from 1982 onward.[95] The "pro-capitalist" aspect of antisemitism, which is far from insignificant, and which is reflected not least in its anti-communism and enthusiasm for competition and "selection," has no place in the Postonean worldview.

Horkheimer and Adorno's reflections succeed, at least to some extent, in what Ulrich Enderwitz rightly accused Postone of seriously neglecting: they grasp antisemitism, "in the context of the historical development of a bourgeois society characterized by social fragmentation and class struggle, as a succession of strategies for suppressing, channeling, and repurposing the social conflicts resulting from such class struggle."[96]

---

94 Postone 1979, p. 11.
95 It only reappeared in a version that incorporated all previous versions — see Postone 2005, p. 165–194.
96 Our translation — Enderwitz 1993.

"... without at the same time attacking capital as such, for to do this would jeopardize the foundations of our national independence."

In Postone's account, and even more so in the his disciples' narratives, antisemitism appears as an anti-capitalist reflex spontaneously emerging from an undifferentiated society. However, antisemitic sources rather confirm the reflections of the original Frankfurt School philosophers. The so-called "Kaiser book" [*Kaiserbuch*] for example — originally titled *Wenn ich der Kaiser wär* and published by Heinrich Claß in 1912 under the pseudonym Daniel Frymann — is an early text linking modern, *völkisch* antisemitism to capitalism. At the time of writing, Claß was the chairman of the Pan-German League and, as Reinhard Opitz notes, a "political advocate of the interests of the biggest Ruhr corporations."[97] He paints a bleak picture of his time. After the unification of the German Empire in 1871, he writes, industry grew at a tremendous pace. In order to meet its labor needs, it had to "bring in foreign nationals of alien blood [*fremdvölkische Ausländer*]."[98] Although industry and its leaders cannot be blamed, the damage is done: a materialistic view of life prolif-

---

97   Opitz 1996, p. 31.
98   Claß 1935, p. 29.

erates in the big cities; we are witnessing moral degeneration, physical decay, the birth of fewer and less vigorous children,[99] the strength of the people waning, race-mixing etc. — and finally, "the massive concentration of unpropertied, poorly educated people in small geographical areas," which makes them vulnerable to "political slogans." "The urban worker is [...] defenselessly exposed to the influence of socialist incitement in speech and in writing. He sees wealth and opulence and compares it to his own situation, and he follows agitators who promise him a better lot in a future state" — i.e., the Social Democrats.[100] The development of capitalist production has an inherent tendency to undermine its own foundations.

It is only then that Claß turns his attention to the Jews. According to him, most Germans were slow to adapt to the new world of modern big capital. The Jews, on the other hand, who on account of their race could not help but subject their "lives to expediency," knew how to *use* these new conditions *for themselves*. They were now able to advance their skills and thus *attain* leading positions in trade and finance. They brought the aspects of haste, recklessness and moral insensitivity into economic life. Claß does not lament "capitalism," nor does he complain about

99   "And who will fill the ranks of our regiments?" Claß asks with
       concern — Claß 1935, p. 32.
100   Our translation — Claß 1935, pp. 29–30.

44

trade or finance. He laments Jewish "abuse of power"[101] — i.e., the exploitation of circumstances originally created by people who "cannot be blamed."

Kurt Fiedler makes a similar argument in *Der Betrug des Marxismus* (*The Marxist Deception*, 1942). The doctrine that surplus-value is a deduction from wages, he writes, is the most audacious incitement to class struggle. He bemoans that Marxism is not interested in the creative achievement of the entrepreneur, nor in the fact that the "entrepreneurial personality" invests wealth in the service of the people or in the risks he takes in the process.[102]

> To honor the innumerable big and small pioneers in the development of German technology and economy — just think of Friedrich Krupp, Carl Friedrich Benz, Gottlieb Daimler, Ernst Abbe, Siemens, Harkort, Borsig and thousands of others — it must be said [...] that they sacrificed themselves in the service of their creative idea and for the sake of their people, and that they lived and created out of joy in their work. Jewish greed was never once the driving force. [...] Much less did these German men ever think of obtaining "profit" and money in a genuinely Jewish manner, i.e. by dark underhand means, by "centralizing," by robbing others of their hard-earned property, or by way of dark and fraudulent manipulations.[103]

---

101   Opitz 1996, p. 31.
102   *Nota bene*, the "risk taken" in the deployment of wealth is the bourgeois legitimation of the interest rate!
103   Our translation — Fiedler 1942, pp. 40–41.

Fiedler stresses that all misery is the result of the "Jewish manipulation of capitalism."[104] It is not capitalism with its "abstract" modes of circulation and commerce that is the problem. After all, "there are also Aryan loans and Aryan competition," Fiedler proudly reports, "which are today being realized in the National-Socialist Greater German Reich."[105] That these did not differ significantly from their allegedly Jewish-abused versions is evidenced by the business practices of the [German] banks during the "Aryanization" of "Jewish commercial enterprises."[106] When pointing its finger at an ominous "golden international," antisemitism, in its ostensibly anti-capitalist aspects, primarily provides an ideological compensation for the very real relations of exploitation, domination and subordination.[107] It is not an irrational reflex to an actually existing "abstract," but a displacement of these relations of exploitation and power/subordination into the beyond, as it were — or in Franz Naumann's words, a "substitute for the

---

104   Fiedler 1942, p. 16.
105   Fiedler 1942, p. 30.
106   See Hilberg 1985, p. 94 et seq.
107   "Golden international" is an antisemitic term that refers to international finance capital, which is allegedly dominated by Jews. The term first appeared in nineteenth-century antisemitic writings by Ottomar Beta and Adolf Stoecker and was later revived by the Nazi economist Gottfried Feder — Translator.

class struggle."[108] To uniformly subsume all the linguistic twists and turns employed by antisemitic and reactionary authors into the categories "concrete" and "abstract" and then interpret them as "anti-capitalist" does not help in our quest to understand and effectively fight antisemitism.

Antisemitism in its essence is in no way a unilateral "attack on the abstract value dimension." To be sure, one may be able to find many examples for the rejection of legal "abstraction" in the Nazi debate about a "new German common law." One can probably also find texts that do not deem the German civil code, which was relatively new at the time, to be the work of men "who at the turn of the century, with the greatest patriotic devotion, united all German tribes into a uniform legal system through the work they created in the field of private law,"[109] but rather consider it in some way "spiritually Jewish." We can safely assume that money *per se* was dubbed a "Jewish invention" somewhere or other. The Young Conservative Ferdinand Fried, at any rate, published lengthy polemics against the rule of "numbers, which are so dreadfully objective and abstract."[110] But that can't be what

108   Naumann 2009, p. 125.
109   Schlegelberger 1937, p. 16.
110   The moniker "Young Conservatives" (*Jungkonservative*) refers to an early trend within the spectrum of German far-right thinkers and societies that emerged from 1918 and retrospectively became known as the "conservative revolution" — Translator.

Postone had in mind: in his theory, the Jews represent the *concretization* of the abstract — and if "the abstract" itself is identified as abstract, without mediation, we are consequently not dealing with cases of antisemitism. By the way: Marx and Engels already noted in the *Communist Manifesto* that value is not actually the issue when "philosophical nonsense" is employed to rail against the rule of the "category of the general" [*das abstrakte Allgemeine*] — the French socialists clearly articulated what the issue really ought to be: the "bourgeois state."[111]

Antisemites only have an ostensible issue with "capitalism." Hitler wrote in *Mein Kampf*: "The absolute separation of stock-exchange capital from the economic life of the nation would make it possible to oppose the process of internationalization in German business without at the same time attacking capital as such, for to do this

---

111   Marx 2002, p. 249. *Abstrakte Allgemeine* [category of the general] refers to Hegel's thus-named theoretical category. The relevant passage in the *Communist Manifesto* reads, "For instance, beneath the French criticism of the economic functions of money, they wrote 'Alienation of Humanity' and beneath the French criticism of the bourgeois State they wrote, 'Dethronement of the Category of the General', and so forth" — *ibid*. The original German version reads: "Z.B. hinter die französische Kritik der Geldverhältnisse schrieben sie „Entäußerung des menschlichen Wesens", hinter die französische Kritik des Bourgeoisstaates schrieben sie „Aufhebung der Herrschaft des abstrakten Allgemeinen" usw." — Translator.

Michael Sommer

would jeopardize the foundations of our national independence."[112] Antisemitism in its "anti-capitalist" aspects is
not anti-capitalist in any sense. On the contrary, it neutral-
izes anti-capitalism and makes the "invocation of the people compatible with the economic rule of big capital."[113]

This is no less true for the present, as Hendrik Puls has
shown with respect to the German National-Democratic
Party's (NPD) social and economic policy as a whole: "If we
speak of an 'anti-capitalism from the right,'" he stresses, "we
run the great risk of obfuscating [the] pro-capitalist content
of the NPD's positions."[114] Postone and his followers believe
that antisemitism fails to challenge capitalism because it mere-

112   Hitler 1939, p. 171.
113   Our translation — thus an apt formulation in Haug, W.F.
       2007, "Annäherung an die faschistische Modalität des Ideo-
       logischen" in *Projekt Ideologietheorie; Faschismus und Ideologie*,
       Hamburg: Argument, pp. 99–100. See in this context also the
       comments in the *Brown Book* of 1934: "The *Völkischer Beo-
       bachter* of April 2nd proclaims the 'spontaneous rise of prices
       on the Stock Exchange, now rid of Jews,' as the most obvious
       result of the boycott movement. We know why such a point
       is made of this; it is to show that the fight is not against the
       existing system, not against capitalism and not even against
       the excesses of capitalism, but that it is a competitive fight
       of the national profiteers against the Jewish profiteers. The
       members of the Stock Exchange can do business even on a
       'Stock Exchange now rid of Jews.' The fight is not against pri-
       vate property, but against the small man; against the 'Aryan'
       workers and middle class who are being hoaxed; against the
       Jewish employees and small traders, who are being ruined."
       — Marley et al 1933, pp. 270–71.
114   Puls 2012, p. 116. The National-Democratic Party serves as
       an umbrella for neo-Nazism and other trends of the German
       extreme right. In recent years, it has lost in significance due to
       the rise of Alternative for Germany (AfD) — Translator.

ly attacks misconceived concretizations of "abstract" forms. But in fact, the exact opposite is true: antisemitism leaves capitalism unchallenged precisely because it does not confront the actual relations of domination and subordination. Thus, antisemitism was able to flourish because it was "linked to interests, as ideology, without conflict."[115] And that is why "those who claim that the critique of the finance sector, the demand for nationalization, or even the breakup of systemic banks feed into antisemitic resentment" are not "fighting antisemitism, but falling for its anti-capitalist rhetoric."[116]

Finally, and only in passing, it is worth stressing how little the thesis of a "hatred for the abstract" does justice to antisemitism also in other respects. This is evident, for instance, in the sheer heterogeneity of antisemitism's depictions of "the Jews" — and we are citing this aspect only as a *pars pro toto* for all kinds of simplified and reductive interpretations of antisemitism. The Postoneans only see the elegant, civilized "Jud' Süß" who dupes dumb peasants with his arithmetic tricks. The dirty, beast-like "eternal Jew" who transmits diseases and lives in a "bug-ridden hole" is missing from their theory of antisemitism, as is the "black-haired Jewish youth" — the sex offender who "lies

115   Our translation — Bloch 1962, p. 247.
116   Our translation — Wetzel 2010.

in wait" for the unsuspicious German girl in order to take her honor.[117] No less ahistorical is the notion that in 1933, "people" who did not understand the "abstract value dimension" assumed power in Germany and set up a kind of special-purpose society for the "destruction of value" — which involved rearmament, a world war, an extensive system of occupation and plunder, and, finally, bureaucratically organized mass extermination.

At the end of the day, the multifaceted nature of antisemitism, which made it attractive and relatable to so many people and served many purposes, is far better captured by Friedrich Hollaender's chanson "An allem sind die Juden schuld" ("The Jews are to blame for everything") than it is by the Postoneans:

> Whether it thunders, whether it rains,
> Whether it snows, whether it hails,
> Whether it's dry, whether it's wet,
> Whether it's cold, whether you sweat,
> Whether it's sunny, whether there's clouds,
> Whether it thaws, whether it pours,
> Whether it drizzles, whether it trickles,
> Whether you cough, whether you sneeze:
> The Jews are to blame for everything![118]

---

117   See Hitler 1939, p. 254.
118   Our translation — a 1931 performance of the song by Annemarie Hase can be heard online at https://www.youtube.com/watch?v=EhKtQASpbY0.

"A growing threat to managers and bankers"

The use of the terms "abstract" and "concrete" has become indiscriminate and tentative among Potstone's disciples. Their reflections may superficially appear as if they were deeply rooted in Marx's work — but in fact, they have little to do with Marx's well-founded, sophisticated system of concepts such as value and use-value, capital and labor, and so on. To return to the word clusters we cited at the beginning, from traditionally brewed beer to the interest economy, all they really are is an arbitrary collection of analogies and "free associations of concepts." Often, one cannot help feeling that they are merely "projections of antisemitic connotations [...] onto the matter at hand."[119] Why "chopping wood" is supposed to be more "concrete" than the activity of a fund manager is not rationally explainable — from the perspective of capital, both are concretely useful labor. Whether "people" might be able to understand one more easily than the other is neither here nor there. The abstract/concrete couplet has undergone a peculiar turn: while for Postone it was at least the result of an analy-

---

119   Hanloser 2011.

sis, however dubious, his disciples use it as an arbitrary guide to tell "good" from "bad."

This method of "free association of concepts," absurd in and of itself, wields enormous consequences. For the Postoneans, forms of social organization are forms of "abstract power" — they are purely autonomous forms that are not located within social relations. This is the conception of capitalism on which their theory on antisemitism is based. "In the antisemitic mind, the Jews are the personifications of abstractness — biologically determined value," emphasizes the Postonean Stephan Grigat.[120] To him and his ilk, antisemitism invariably appears as the necessarily doomed attempt to overcome the inherent laws of capitalist societies within actual social relations. From there, however, it is only a small step to smear any social protest as "actually" antisemitic. The target of protest no longer even needs to be specifically "suitable" to personify "the abstract."

Case in point: "In March," as one blogger reported in 2009, "a group of 'angry workers' protesting the closure of their workplace in France kidnapped a manager and locked him up — but released him after a few hours. More recently, [Left Party politician] Oskar Lafontaine drew attention when endorsing the assault on the French man-

---

120   Grigat 1999.

ager and predicting social unrest. In a thoroughly ominous fashion, the crisis is thus making its presence felt. The ideology of hatred for the abstract is gaining new popularity, and — most importantly — it is being put into practice." This, the author concludes, implies "a growing threat [...] for managers and bankers."[121]

While in France, "bossnapping" — i.e., workers locking up factory managers in order to lend weight to their demands — is a popular subject of satire, in Germany "resistance against the encroachments of capital"[122] is likened to the antisemitism that culminated in the destruction of the European Jews and thus made into something that must be prevented at all costs. It is hard to decide which is more obnoxious: the comparison itself or the reverse implication that Auschwitz was somehow comparable to locking an entrepreneur in the factory cafeteria overnight.

In the last analysis, Postone devotees lay "a protective hand over the 'character masks' of capitalism and its institutions — although this favour hasn't even been requested."[123] Is this, as Ulrich Enderwitz contemplates in his Postone critique, by definition liberalism, the "attempt of

---

121   Our translation — the German blog was published on May 3, 2009, at the now defunct address http://schildkroete.blog-sport.de/2009/05/03/der-hass-aufs-abstrakte/.

122   See Marx 1865, chapter 3.

123   Hanloser 2011.

the enlightened bourgeois to criticize the political system without undermining the economic basis of the system from which the bourgeoisie profits"? Or is this the work of a left which, because it has failed for the foreseeable future, has turned its back on the critique of capital, which it nonchalantly takes for granted as well as regards as completed (thus only showing itself to be the alter ego of liberalism)?[124] Ultimately, it makes no difference because the result is the same: it is no longer exploitation and the quest for profit that are perceived as the problem, but the "people," who "cannot understand" the "mysterious intangibility, abstractness and universality" of the value dimension. For this left, the world-historical adversaries are no longer capitalism and its extreme form, fascism, on one side, and the anti-capitalist movement on the other. Instead, it is capitalism, glorified as "modernity" and "civilization" par excellence, contending against the anti-capitalist fascist mass movement.

While Postone at least notes that the "hatred of the abstract" is the flipside of "liberal thought, where the "domination of the abstract remains unquestioned,"[125] his disciples do not make a great fuss about such trifles: their

---

124   Enderwitz 1993.
125   Postone 1986.

"anti-fascism," which targets the "hatred of the abstract" and is "fully compatible with (neo) liberalism," ultimately comes down to a "pro-capitalist hymn to the world" which, with its "globalization, market relations and unemployment, is just the way it is."[126]

"The fundamental lie of those who actually do not want to help"

So why the enduring popularity of the "doctrine" of "hatred of the abstract"? Its critique, which has "congealed into jargon,"[127] suits a left that after 1990 gave up on any real possibility of social change. For this left, this "Marxist theory of antisemitism" is highly attractive: it allows you to deem yourself at the forefront of critical consciousness without ever having to talk about the working class or class struggle. On the contrary, you can denounce the "common rabble" as scarred by fetishistic relations. Without ever coming into conflict with the powerful in society, indeed while standing by their side, you can save face as an anti-fascist critic. The professional ideologues of this society have long since understood this.[128]

---

126 Hanloser 2012.
127 Our translation — Hanloser 2011.
128 Wolf Lotter: "Das Gute und die Bösen" in *brand eins* of September 2011, p. 48.

Michael Sommer

"Antisemitism and anti-capitalism march to the same steady drum beat" is how Bernd Ziesemer summed up Postone's essay in the German business newspaper *Handelsblatt*, where he celebrated this as a noteworthy insight.[129] And the business magazine *brand eins* has long since declared as a matter of course that "for long periods in history" it had been "impossible to separate" antisemitism from anti-capitalism.

Capitalist society is no longer criticized as a system of "enslavement" and "servitude" (as Marx called it)[130] that must be changed, dismantled and transformed by means of genuine social struggle into a social life process subjected to the conscious, systematic control of freely associated individuals. Postone writes: "Any 'anticapitalism' which seeks the immediate negation of the abstract and glorifies the concrete — instead of practically and theoretically considering what the historical overcoming of both could mean — can, at best, be socially and politically impotent in the face of capital. At worst it can be dangerous, even if the needs it expresses could be interpreted as emancipatory."[131] To call for an anti-capitalism that not only abolishes

---

129   Bernd Ziesemer: 'Antikapitalismus und Antisemitismus' in
       Handelsblatt of 13 May 2005.
130   Marx 1990, p. 875.
131   Postone 1979, p. 14.

value as an expression of the unconsciousness [*Unbewusstheit*] of social relations, but also overcomes the "concrete" — use value, production, etc. — is to denounce any serious anti-capitalism, indeed even the most timid critique of capitalism, as "hatred of the abstract" and thus as potential or actual "antisemitism."

Only human beings can transform and reshape the conditions that they themselves have created. As correct as it is to say that capitalist production as a whole is beyond the reach of the individual, it is also true that only people can put an end to the inherent dynamics of its intertwined, interlocking structures of movement and abolish the existing, historically conditioned laws of capital. This liberation from self-induced, self-inflicted natural limitations comes to pass as the economic-social relations that appear in forms of value are abolished — Marx and Engels recommended to start with "despotic inroads on the rights of property."[132] Such a process of dismantling social relations is also an active creative process: it consists in the transformation and reorganization of economic and social relations, drawing on emancipatory and civilizational tendencies that are already present and advancing them further.[133]

---

132   Marx and Engels 2002, p. 243.
133   See also Sommer and Wolf 2008, p. 159.

On the long road that leads us there, people may not always get to the root of the problem. They might moralize or provide a mere patchwork of partial solutions; this is where the left comes into play. But from the point of view of Postone's epigones in the discourse on antisemitism and fascism, as well as sections of the present-day left, especially the antifa movement, such efforts at liberation at best amount to cases of a misguided and dangerous "concretization of the abstract." For them, Max Horkheimer's words hold true:

> All or Nothing: Be mistrustful of the person who says that unless everyone is helped, it's no use. That is the fundamental lie of those who actually do not want to help and hide behind a theory to excuse their failure to do their duty in a concrete case. They rationalize their inhumanity. There is a resemblance between them and the devout: both preserve their good conscience by pleading 'higher' considerations when they abandon you to your helplessness.[134]

However, the difference between those who do not want to do anything (unless they can tackle the totality of existing relations all at once) and the Postoneans is that the former merely abandon you. The Postone-trained "anti-fascists," on the other hand, will "in a concrete

---

134   Horkheimer 1978, p. 35.

case" defend capital and denounce anyone who protests against the power of corporations as a Nazi who must be stopped. That is about the last thing anti-fascism needs to do today.

Appendix: "The abstraction principle projected in a Manichean fashion onto Judaism" — A Greatest Hits Compilation

Postone's text has played an important role in the antisemitism and fascism discourse of significant sections of the German left, especially in the antifa movement. To understand and apply his theses is regarded by many as tantamount to engaging in the highest levels of left-wing thinking — as we have seen, wrongly. We shall illustrate the consequences of this mistaken belief with a compilation of some of the most egregious gaffes and bloomers. The order of the passages presented below will follow that of the preceding essay: we will start from general reflections on Marx's theory in *Capital*, then move on to Postone's interpretations and finally arrive at the political conclusions drawn by his disciples. The opacity and linguistic inadequacies of these text samples have a very peculiar comic effect. However, their abstruseness should not worry the reader too much. There is not a lot to understand here. The tragedy is precisely that these concoctions are still taken seriously, that their feigned scientificity enjoys any respect at all. The following examples testify to the depressing state of important fields of left-wing and anti-fascist debate in the Germanophone countries.

Any critique of capitalism that fails to address the fetishism of the commodity is nothing more than a fetishized perception of society that cannot capture or explain it. It is indispensable at this point to examine the fetish character in more detail. To do so, we must look at the commodity, this "thing which transcends sensuousness," more closely. If you look at a table, it is a table. However, if the table is a commodity, i.e. made for exchange, it breaks down [sic — Translator] into two parts: exchange-value and use-value. The thing — the commodity — thus has a double character. While use-value remains visible as something concrete, exchange-value appears only in the abstract mediation of exchange and conceals that which determines it. In the perception of the commodity as pure use-value, exchange value (i.e. the value), appears as a natural property of the commodity rather than as a product of expended labor (time), i.e. as a social relation.[1]

---

1   Our translation — the original German text is available from Copy Riot at https://copyriot.com/lili/texte/antisem.html.

Elsewhere we read:

[...] it is useful to be familiar with Marx's theory of the fetish character of commodities, which addresses the difference between the essence and the appearance of capitalist relations and is fundamental for establishing a historical epistemology. Marx analyzes commodities, money, and capital not only as economic forms, but also as social forms of relations. Commodities have a "double character": exchange-value and use-value. "By equating their different products to each other in exchange as values, they equate their different kinds of labour as human labour." It is therefore through value that a social relation is reified in every product of labor. Therefore, labor does not only become concrete when it produces a useful thing — it also has an abstract character. Because the human labor expended is equated in commodity exchange, the usefulness of a commodity (use-value) is no longer the primary value-determining factor. Rather, the exchange-value now determines the value of commodities as a result of a relationship of equivalence. Thus, under capitalism, these commodities are no longer produced only for practical use, but for commodity exchange from the outset. Hence, possession of commodities now also means wealth. Likewise, exchange-value always fluctuates in dependence on market relations and consolidates itself outside the control of the exchanger or producer. Thus, labor also acquires a "double character" in that it is commodity-producing, concrete labor as well as value-producing, abstract labor.[2]

---

2   Our translation — the original German text is available at http://aargb.blogsport.de/texte/30antisemitismus/der-moderne-antisemitismus-als-form-von-antikapitalismus/.

"A knife which fails to cut, a piece of thread which keeps on snapping, forcibly remind us of Mr A, the cutler, or Mr B, the spinner," Marx wrote in *Capital, Volume I*. The table that "breaks down into two parts" appears in a text entitled "Reflections on the continuity of antisemitism on the German left." However, just like Michaela Müller's discovery of a "use-value" that is not a "primary value-determining factor" (namely in her article "Modern antisemitism as a form of anti-capitalism"), the broken table forcibly reminds us not of the clumsy carpenter C, but of the fact that you don't really need to know your Marx all that well to feign gravity and importance in the field of Marxist antisemitism theory. But let us continue:

> Since the abstract is experienced as threatening and incomprehensible, it is demonized, just as the concrete is idolized and seen as natural. This is also reflected in the valorization of physical labor as "productive labor," while the capitalist level of mediation and everything associated with it is devalued.[3]

> Postone views antisemitism as a fetish, as a personification of the abstract part of capitalist society that is segregated along with the Jews.[4]

---

3   Our translation — Ingo Seidel's original German text, "Die Abstraktion des Marktes" ("The abstraction of the market"), is available at http://www.antisemitismus.net/theorie/kritische-theorie/042.htm.

4   Keller, Kögler, Krawinkel and Schlemermayer 2011, p. 139.

Michael Sommer

Because Postone's text is so vague and tentative, it is actually hard to misrepresent. Just as long as you use the right terms — concrete, abstract, fetish, Jews — it will be alright somehow. Yet sometimes, the results can be pretty absurd:

> The exterminatory antisemitism and racism of the neo-Nazis must be viewed as a special form of "anti-capitalism" since they reduce capitalism to the sphere of circulation, which is personified by the Jews or non-Germans, who end up in the national community [*Volksgemeinschaft*] or in an agrarian or corporative state.[5]

The "sphere of circulation" is personified by "non-Germans" — who then end up in a corporative state. Is this satire or serious contribution to the debate? Frankfurt antifa truly don't make it easy for us.

> [...] in the antisemitic imagination, Jews have become the symbol for the abstract *per se* [...] the dichotomy between worldliness and rootedness in the soil [...]. Moishe Postone has described it thus: the value-form of modern society and the resulting differentiation between use-value and exchange-value, on the one hand, and the fetishization of commodities, on the other, are the reason that antisemitism links these economic spheres to a concretist worldview in which the abstraction principle is projected in a Manichean fashion onto Judaism.[6]

---

5   Our translation — see https://www.antifa-frankfurt.org/Mai2002/VoelkischerAntikapitalismus.html.

6   Our translation — Samuel Salzborn: 'Wahn der Homogenität. Zur politischen Theorie des Antisemitismus. Eine Skizze' (The delusion of homogeneity. On the political theory of antisemitism. A draft) in *Jungle World* of April 22, 2010, avail-

This enigmatic sentence was published in a *Jungle World* article authored by Samuel Salzborn, Professor of Social Sciences at the Georg August University of Göttingen.[7]

His "Marxism," according to which the value-form of modern society results in a differentiation between use-value and exchange-value, is already impressive enough. It is far surpassed, however, by his "Postoneanism." Marx never spoke of an outright "abstraction principle" in connection with commodity, value, capital and fetish — not even Postone did that. Salzborn has so far not revealed the source from which he had derived this term. He probably introduced it on his own accord just because it sounded theoretically meaningful to him.

It is astonishing, though — or more precisely, revealing of Salzborn's scientific unseriousness — what he does *not* write: in fact, Nazi civil law scholars had proclaimed it a key objective in the creation of a new "People's Code" [*Volksgesetzbuch*] to abolish the principle of abstraction — that is, the principle of legal independence of the conveyance on sale [*Erfüllungsgeschäft*] from the contract of

---

able at https://jungle.world/artikel/2010/16/wahn-der-homogenitaet.

7   At the time of translating in 2021, Samuel Salzborn was the Anti-Semitism Commissioner of the State of Berlin and Adjunct Professor of Political Science at the Justus Liebig University in Giessen — Translator

sale [*Verpflichtungsgeschäft*], which is central to the German civil code — in favor of a "causal" property transfer.[8] They argued that the abstraction principle was alien to the national and popular character, inequitable, not up to date, derived from historicism and liberalism, and so on. The Nazi debate was quite controversial, but more or less petered out when it was decided that the code of law was not, at the end of the day, meant to serve as a "reader for national comrades [*Volksgenossen*]," but as a tool for the "guardians of the law" to enforce it. So much for "popular character"...

Later debates in the GDR, as well as the far-reaching abrogation of the abstraction principle from the civil code of the country, were motivated mainly by the publication of *Die historische Bedingtheit der Abstraktion von der causa* by the lawyer Hans Kleine in 1953. Kleine had made generous use of a 1940 paper on the history of the abstraction principle, but called for the abolition of abstraction from the causa on the grounds that the conditions of its existence — a weak bourgeoisie under semi-feudal conditions

---

8   "Causa" is a comprehensive term for any proceeding in a court of law whereby an individual seeks a legal remedy. In a "causal" property transfer, the contract of sale itself is capable of transferring the property rights where the parties so intend, and invalidity of the contract of sale can invalidate the property transfer, as in French and English law, as to the sale of movables — Translator

in Prussia — had been overcome, and that this legal institution was no longer needed under socialist conditions.

It would be highly interesting to trace these discussions and developments in a critical materialist fashion. But Salzborn does not even notice this.

> As capital, value possesses the most extreme form of abstractness and mobility. Now, people try to capture this abstractness in the Jews. They do not regard the Jews themselves as immediate abstractness and mobility, but — on account of the fact that value, which has no tangible substance, requires use-value as a material cover, and because the concrete character of the commodity are expressed only through the abstract character of money — they perceive them as the material carriers of abstractness.[9]

> One of the features of modern antisemitism is the perception of capitalism as divided into two separate spheres: the sphere of production is perceived as concrete and is often eulogized, while the sphere of exchange and finance is perceived as abstract and is blamed for all the negative consequences of capitalism. In antisemitic thinking, the abstract side of capitalism is associated with the Jews.[10]

> Postone identifies a connection between the historical theory of a materialistic form [sic — Translator]. Thus, the Jews personified the rapid development of industrial capitalism. They were perceived as carriers for money. The commod-

---

9   Our translation — Grigat 2002.
10   Our translation — Ulrike Becker: "The German obsession with work and antisemitism" in *Trend Onlinezeitung* at http://www.trend.infopartisan.net/trd1200/t091200.html.

ity (money) has a "double character." Value and use-value. At the time, Jews were thought to possess power that assumed the form of a material carrier, the commodity. Postone says that the capitalist, social relations [sic — Translator] find their expression in the abstract dimension, such as money and external, abstract, universal "laws." Therefore, capitalist social relations must be described as antinomic, as an opposition between the abstract and the concrete. The concrete side (Aryan) appears as pure material nature and the abstract side (Jew) appears in the form of "objective" natural laws.[11]

Yes, Postone must have said something like that. But, as is usually the case, there isn't much left of it except jargon.

[...] Antisemitism, which after Auschwitz cannot present itself in its pure form (yet) [...] reappears in [...] that vague and paranoid sense of threat, be it by the environmental toxins invoked by the German ecological movement, or by nuclear world powers, the scourge of the German peace movement; [...] in any attempt to play off a concrete against an abstract — a mode of argumentation that, as Moishe Postone has shown, operates within an antinomy instead of completely abandoning it as a paradigm; and in agitation against the "world of neon, concrete and plastic" that was so popular in the seventies and eighties — against all that is artificial and manufactured.[12]

---

11   Our translation — Eva Pasternak: *Antisemitismus und Natio-nalsozialismus. Postones Thesen und Begründungen zum Thema Antisemitismus und Nationalsozialismus*, seminar paper, Google Books preview available at https://www.google.ca/books/edition/Antisemitismus_und_Nationalsozialismus/gVd3QI0DyngC?hl=en&gbpv=0.
12   Our translation — Fabian Kettner: *Volksgemeinschaft und Antisemitismus*, available from Rote Ruhr Uni at https://www.rote-ruhr-uni.com/texte/kettner_volksgemeinschaft_und_

Gerhard Hanloser noted as early as 2005:

> Here, association takes the place of analysis, and it is alarming how quickly critics of "structural antisemitism" react to mere words like Pavlov's dog. This only shows the degree to which people and groups particularly from the so-called "anti-German" milieu are themselves driven by antisemitic associations. Why is the mere use of words such as "vagabond" or "subversive" — to cite further examples — supposed to be antisemitic? What idea of the "Jew" (even the identification of people as such is supposedly antisemitic) do the critics of "structural antisemitism" themselves have when admonishing these words? Decrying such terms as "structurally antisemitic" says more about the pseudo-critics than it does about the object of criticism.[13]

Say no more.

> Whoever plays off the concrete and abstract sides of capitalism against each other is committing a mistake, in my opinion. That can sometimes happen, and it isn't something one couldn't calmly discuss.[14]

That's what it says in "Antisemitism and critique of capitalism" over at the *Emanzipation oder Barberei* blog. So it's not end of the world, after all? Well, it is:

> Solidarity with Israel is not an end in itself, but flows from the immediate danger posed by antisemitism. Its ex-

---

antisemitismus.shtml.
13   Our translation — Hanloser 2005.
14   Our translation — original German text available from *Emanzipation oder Barbarei* at http://emanzipationoderbarbarei. blogsport.de/2012/02/19/antisemitismus-und-kapitalis-muskritik/.

istence is caused by a flawed analysis of capitalism, which leads to a resentful anti-capitalism. Its essential feature is the fetishistic distinction between good (concrete) and bad (abstract) phenomena of the capitalist production and valorization process. Abstract phenomena, such as the interest economy, are projected onto the Jews and naturalized, while concrete phenomena (for example, chopping wood, baking bread rolls, or "honest" work in general) are conceived as virtuous activities. However, the two processes are not understood as a capitalist totality. Antisemitism is therefore not a form of racism, but an all-encompassing formula that seeks to explain the world.[15]

Baking bread rolls and the interest economy are not understood as a capitalist totality — therefore: solidarity with Israel! You think that's absurd? Read on:

The equation x commodity A = y commodity B, this nucleus of fetishism — a perception and practice that is at once wrong and right, as criticized by Marx at the very beginning of *Capital* — compares two equally large quanta of expended abstract human labor. Thus, according to Marx, use-value becomes the form of appearance of its opposite, value. The opposition between abstract and concrete is already articulated in this innocuous-looking equation, which can only be adequately criticized if its historical and contemporary implications are taken into account. This opposition between the abstract and the concrete is materialized

---

15   Our translation — original German text available from Bundesarbeitskreis Shalom (Shalom Working Group, the pro-Israel organization operating in the youth league of the German Left Party, Die Linke) at http://bak-shalom.de/index.php/bildung/warum-solidaritat-mit-israel/.

today not least in the State of Israel, which is artificial in the best sense of the word, and the blood-and-soil intifada of the Palestinians, for which the majority of the anti-globalization movement and the peace movement serve as auxiliaries. [...] Those who want to criticize the formula x commodity A = y commodity B in all its consequences instead of engaging with it only tenuously must declare their solidarity with the armed self-defense of Israel.[16]

Stephan Grigat, at the time of writing a lecturer at the Faculty of Jewish Studies at the Institute for Political Science and the Institute for Philosophy of the University of Vienna, as well as co-founder and scientific director of the "Stop the Bomb" campaign in Austria,[17] emerges as the true "perfector of the Postone school" — more still than the "Shalom Working Group" in the Left Party quoted earlier. In a chain of rather free associations, he summarily transforms "the Palestinians" into revenants of SS units driven by exterminatory antisemitic ideology. For him, solidarity with Israel's armed "self-defense" follows almost automatically from Marx's analysis of the value-form (by now, everybody will know the chant frequently heard at

---

16   Grigat 2003.
17   Stop the Bomb is an NGO that seeks to prevent Iran from acquiring nuclear weapons. Although it nominally promotes tougher sanctions and diplomatic isolation, critics have accused it of warmongering against Iran. The campaign has thus earned itself the derisory nickname Drop the Bomb — Translator

German street demonstrations, "IDF in Ramallah — that's the real antifa!"). Ultimately, it's probably true what has been said about Postone-inspired antisemitism theory, albeit not in the intended sense: These are "just about the most strenuous mental contortions hitherto demanded of left-wing thinking."

BIBLIOGRAPHY

Bloch, Ernst 1962, *Subjekt-Objekt. Erläuterungen zu Hegel*, Frankfurt: Suhrkamp.

Claß, Heinrich 1935 [1912], *Das Kaiserbuch*, Berlin: Verlag der Vermögensverwaltung des Alldeutschen Verbandes.

Claussen, Detlev 1988, *Vom Judenhass zum Antisemitismus. Materialien einer verleugneten Geschichte*, Darmstadt: Luchterhand.

——— 2005, *Grenzen der Aufklärung. Die gesellschaftliche Genese des modernen Antisemitismus*, Frankfurt: Fischer-Taschenbuch-Verlag.

Enderwitz, Ulrich 1993, "Linker Strukturalismus. Einige Überlegungen zu Postones Antisemitismus-Thesen" in *Kritik und Krise* 6, Freiburg: ça ira Verlag. Available from ça ira at https://www.ca-ira.net/verlag/leseproben/ulrich-enderwitz-linker-strukturalismus-2/

——— 2005, *Konsum, Terror und Gesellschaftskritik. Eine Tour d'horizon*, Münster: Unrast Verlag.

Michael Sommer

Engels, Frederick 1868, "Review of Volume One of *Capital* for
The Fortnightly Review," available from Marxists.org at
https://www.marxists.org/archive/marx/works/1867/
reviews-capital/fortnightly.htm

——— 1894, *Herr Eugen Dühring's Revolution in Science*, PDF
available from Marxists.org at https://www.marxists.org/
archive/marx/works/download/pdf/anti_duhring.pdf

Fiedler, Kurt 1942, *Der Betrug des Marxismus*, Leipzig: Lühe.

Grigat, Stephan 1999, "Antisemitismus und Fetischismus.
Kritische Theorie zur Basisideologie der bürgerlichen
Gesellschaft," available from Café Critique at cafecri-
tique.priv.at/fetisch.html

——— 2003, "Der Hass der Antiglobalisierungsbewegung auf
Israel," available from Café Critique at http://www.
cafecritique.priv.at/GrigatSPOG.html

——— 2002, "Logik und Struktur des Antisemitismus. Eine
Einführung," presentation in Frankfurt on 14 May
2002, transcription available from Gruppe ISKRA
at http://iskra.blogsport.de/texte/logik-und-struk-
tur-des-antisemitismus-eine-einfuehrung/

Hanloser, Gerhard 2004, "Verkürzter Antikapitalismus? Zur
Kritik and Postones 'Nationalsozialismus und Antisemitismus'" in *analyse & kritik* 15 October 2004,
also pp. 28-32 in *Buko-Seminar Antisemitismus Reader*, PDF available at https://www.buko.info/filead-
min/user_upload/doc/reader/reader_antisem.pdf

——— 2005, "Kapitalismuskritik und falsche Personalisierung"
in *analyse & kritik* of 21 October 2005.

———— 2011, "ATTAC, The Critique of Globalization, and 'Structural Antisemitism'", available from communism at http://communism.blogsport.eu/2011/07/18/attac-the-critique-of-globalization-and-structural-antisemitism/

———— 2012, "Antikollektivismus. Der neue Geist 'linker' Sozialstaatskritik," available from Trend Onlinezeitung at http://www.trend.infopartisan.net/trd1205/t251205.html

Hilberg, Raul 1985 [1961], *The Destrution of the European Jews*, New York and London: Holmes & Meier.

Hitler, Adolf 1939 [1925], *Mein Kampf* (unexpurgated edition), London, New York and Melbourne: Hurts and Blackett Ltd.

Horkheimer, Max 1978, *Dawn & Decline. Notes 1926-31 and 1950-69*, New York: Seabury Press.

Horkheimer, Max and Theodor Adorno 2002 [1947], *Dialectic of Enlightenment. Philosophical Fragments*, Stanford: Stanford University Press.

Keller, Mirja and Lena Kögler, Moritz Krawinkel and Jan Schlemermeyer 2011, *Antifa. Geschichte und Organisierung*, Stuttgart: Schmetterling-Verlag.

Marley, Dudley Leigh Aman et al 1933, *The Brown Book of the Hitler Terror and the Burning of the Reichstag*, New York: Alfred A. Knopf, Inc. Available from Hathi Trust at https://babel.hathitrust.org/cgi/pt?id=mdp.39015046786375&view=1up&seq=1

Marx, Karl 1846, Letter from Marx to Pavel Vasilyevich Annenkov, available at Marxists.org.

―――― 1857, *Grundrisse*, available at Marxists.org.

―――― 1859, *A Contribution to the Critique of Political Economy*, available at Marxists.org.

―――― 1861-64, "The Process of Production of Capital, Draft Chapter 6 of *Capital*: Results of the Direct Production Process," available from Marxists.org at https://www.marxists.org/archive/marx/works/1864/economic/ch02.htm

―――― 1865, *Value, Price and Profit*, available at marxists.org.

―――― 1867a, "The Commodity — Ch. 1 as per First German Edition" in *Capital. A Critique of Political Economy*, available from Marxists.org at https://www.marxists.org/archive/marx/works/1867-c1/commodity.htm

―――― 1867b, "The Value Form. Appendix to the 1st German edition of *Capital, Volume I*, 1867" in *Capital. A Critique of Political Economy*, available at marxists.org.

―――― 1881, "Notes on Adolph Wagner's *Lehrbuch der politischen Ökonomie* (Second Edition), Volume 1, 1879," available at marxists.org.

―――― 1987 [1871-72], "Ergänzungen und Veränderungen zum ersten Band des 'Kapitals'" in *Marx-Engels Gesamtausgabe (MEGA), Abt. 2. 'Das Kapital' und Vorarbeiten / Karl Marx Bd. 6. Das Kapital, Kritik der politischen Ökonomie, erster Band, Hamburg 1872*, Berlin: Akademie-Verlag.

——— 1987b [1857-58], Second Draft of *Critique of Political Economy* in *Marx-Engels Collected Works*, vol. 29, Moscow: Progress Publishers. Available from HistoryIsAWeapon.org at http://hiaw.org/defcon6/works/1858/economic/draft.html.

——— 1990 [1887], *Capital, Volume I*, London and New York: Penguin.

——— 1991 [1894], *Capital, Volume III*, New York and London: Penguin.

——— 1992 [1885], *Capital, Volume II*, New York and London: Penguin

——— 2015 [1887], *Capital, Volume I*, PDF available from Marxists.org at https://www.marxists.org/archive/marx/works/download/pdf/Capital-Volume-I.pdf

——— 2018 [1871-72], "Die Wertform. Ergänzungen und Veränderungen zum ersten Band des 'Kapitals.' Manuskript (1871/72)" in *Kapital 1.5. Die Wertform*, second edition, Berlin: Klaus Dietz Verlag. PDF available from Dietz at https://dietzberlin.de/wp-content/uploads/2021/01/Kapital_1.5.pdf

Marx, Karl and Frederick Engels 2002 [1848], *The Communist Manifesto*, New York and London: Penguin.

Neumann, Franz 2009 [1944], *Behemoth: The Structure and Practice of National Socialism*, Chicago: Ivan R. Dee.

Opitz, Reinhard 1996, *Faschismus und Neofaschismus*, Cologne: Pahl-Rugenstein Verlag.

Postone, Moishe 1979, "Anti-Semitism and National Socialism," available from the Internet Archive at https://ia802801. us.archive.org/23/items/AntiSemitismAndNationalSo-cialismMoishePostone/Anti-Semitism%20and%20Na-tional%20Socialism%20-%20Moishe%20Postone.pdf

—— 1986, "Anti-Semitism and National Socialism," available from the Anarchist Library at https://theanar-chistlibrary.org/library/moishe-postone-anti-semi-tism-and-national-socialism

—— 1993, *Time, Labor, and Social Domination*, New York: Cambridge University Press. PDF available from Libcom.org at https://libcom.org/files/Moishe%20Postone%20-%20Time,%20Labor,%20and%20So-cial%20Domination.pdf

—— 2005: *Deutschland, die Linke und der Holocaust*, Freiburg: Ça ira.

—— 2006, "History and Helplessness: Mass Mobilization and Contemporary Forms of Anticapitalism," PDF available from the Platypus Affiliated Society at https://platypus1917.org/wp-content/uploads/read-ings/postonemoishe_historyhelplessness.pdf

Puls, Hendrik 2012, *Antikapitalismus von rechts? Wirtschafts- und sozialpolitische Positionen der NPD*, Münster: Edition Assemblage.

Schlegelberger, Franz 1937, *Abschied vom BGB. Vortrag, ge-halten in der Universität zu Heidelberg am 25. Januar 1937*, Berlin: F. Vahlen.

Sommer, Michael and Dieter Wolf 2008, *Imaginäre Bedeutungen und historische Schranken der Erkenntnis. Eine Kritik an Cornelius Castoriadis*, Hamburg: Argument.

Thomas, Martin 2010, "Zionism, anti-semitism and the left. An Interview with Moishe Postone," *Solidarity* 3/166, 4 Feb 2010. Available online on the *Krisis* website at https://www.krisis.org/2010/zionism-anti-semitism-and-the-left/

Weiß, Volker 2005, "Die faschistische Utopie und ihre nationalsozialistische Realisierung" in *Phase2*,16/2005, PDF with excerpts available at http://www.akbp.de/AS_WiSe0607/AS_Weiss_Auszug.pdf

Wetzel Wolf 2010, "Über die Mächtigkeit der Banken (aktualisiert)," available from Wetzel Wolf's blog at https://wolfwetzel.wordpress.com/2010/08/14/14-8-2010-uber-die-machtigkeiten-von-banken/

Wolf, Dieter 2007, "Der Warenfetisch und der Gegensatz von Natur und Geist," PDF available from Dieterwolf.net at http://www.dieterwolf.net/pdf/Warenfetisch-NaturGeist.pdf

Michael Sommer researches Marx's theory of capitalism. In 2008, together with Dieter Wolf, he published a critique of the Greek-French economist and philosopher Cornelius Castoriadis entitled *Imaginäre Bedeutungen und historische Schranken der Erkenntnis*. Together with Susann Witt-Stahl, he edited the volume *"Antifa heisst Luftangriff!" Regression einer revolutionären Bewegung* (2014), in which the text translated for this book was originally published.

Mike Macnair teaches law at St. Hugh's College, Oxford. He is a regular writer for the *Weekly Worker*. He is the author of *Revolutionary Strategy* (2008) and the co-author with Jamie Gough of *Gay Liberation in the 80s* (1985).

Maciej Zurowski is a translator working in German, Polish, and English. He has translated political biographies of Otto Bauer and Ernest Mandel and historical texts by Karl Kautsky, Ernst Niekisch, Clara Zetkin, and others. He has also written for *Melodie und Rhythmus*, *Weekly Worker*, and *Jacobin*.